The Fractured College Prep Pipeline

Hoarding Opportunities to Learn

Heather E. Price

TEACHERS COLLEGE PRESS

TEACHERS COLLEGE | COLUMBIA UNIVERSITY
NEW YORK AND LONDON

Thank you for keeping-up my spirits,
Pete, Mom, and Dad.

Published by Teachers College Press,® 1234 Amsterdam Avenue, New York, NY 10027

Copyright © 2021 by Teachers College, Columbia University

Cover design by adam b. bohannon

Library of Congress Cataloging-in-Publication Data

Names: Price, Heather E. (Heather Elaine), author.
Title: The fractured college prep pipeline : hoarding opportunities to learn /
    Heather E. Price.
Description: New York, NY : Teachers College Press, [2021] |
    Includes bibliographical references and index.
Identifiers: LCCN 2020055837 (print) | LCCN 2020055838 (ebook) |
    ISBN 9780807765036 (hardcover) | ISBN 9780807765029 (paperback) |
    ISBN 9780807779408 (ebook)
Subjects: LCSH: College preparation programs—United States. | Universities
    and colleges—United States—Admission. | Universities and colleges—
    United States—Entrance requirements. | Universities and colleges—
    United States—Examinations.
Classification: LCC LB2351.2 .P75 2021 (print) | LCC LB2351.2 (ebook) |
    DDC 378.1/610973—dc23
LC record available at https://lccn.loc.gov/2020055837
LC ebook record available at https://lccn.loc.gov/2020055838

ISBN 978-0-8077-6502-9 (paper)
ISBN 978-0-8077-6503-6 (hardcover)
ISBN 978-0-8077-7940-8 (ebook)

Printed on acid-free paper
Manufactured in the United States of America

Contents

Prelude

When you read scholarly journal articles, the writing is supposed to be strictly social scientific and right to the point. In teaching, it is common to work with examples and metaphors to help give the abstract ideas shape. Writing a book allows expansion of ideas to explain them to you, the reader, in much in the same way that classes are taught. The writing in this book does this by using four states (Arizona, Florida, Michigan, and North Carolina) as concrete examples, and metaphors help imagine how things work.

The book presentation is like that of a puzzle being put together. Puzzles are not constructed from left to right and top to bottom, but instead they fall into place as different pieces start to make sense in the general outline. In the same way, this presentation is not always in the traditional, linear manner. This isn't meant to confuse, but rather all the pieces will be put together and you will be led through the assembly process.

In putting together this book's puzzle, I will start by assembling the frame of the puzzle and then cluster alike pieces together. Once these clusters find their natural boundaries, they begin to fit together and attach to the frame. By the end, the entire puzzle will portray the full picture of segregated learning that is not unfamiliar in the American education system, but which is taking new shape in this early part of this century, with an opacity that makes it difficult for parents and teachers to see its grip on their students' learning opportunities from the inside of a school system.

Acknowledgments

This project evolved over many years, from my working as a research assistant with Sean Kelly to working in Michigan with David, Jeff, Claire, Lauren, Leah, Edwin, and Sharon to years of conversations with Kristi Donaldson. I am indebted to all of these good people for their ideas, dialogue, and shared enthusiasm around this topic, their expertise, and their perspectives. When Kristi was able find the time to work with me, I was ever so grateful. Her pointed and stimulating feedback on some chapters and her contribution to Chapter 2 were gifts. Her deep knowledge of tracking and unmatched expertise in IB cannot be overstated.

The Center for Research on Educational Opportunity (CREO) at the University of Notre Dame provided a riveting intellectual space to grapple with the ideas of opportunities to learn, and Maureen Hallinan's stamp on this field is forever present. Mark Berends continues to carry the mission of the center forward with great integrity. I never thought that I'd do a project about tracking, and here we are. It's just in our CREO veins.

I am also indebted to the feedback from Adam Pope at University of Arkansas, Brian Ellerbeck at Teachers College Press, and the rigorous manuscript reviewers for their direct and clear feedback. I hope that I executed your suggestions well.

To Pete and my parents. These last few years has seen more hospitals and doctors than we need to remember. Through it, you continued to encourage me to work on this project because you saw a fire in me to get this to the public space. Thank you for all your support.

During the final months of this manuscript, the COVID-19 pandemic broke out and we saw schooling opportunities blast open the gap between schools with and without resources. In the final weeks, the nation erupted in moral outrage for justice for George Floyd and the accumulation of racialized violence in this country. I hope this project complements our social learnings to understand the structurally embedded divides in the United States that have real consequences that can cause great harm or heal deep historical wounds. These structures do not stand neutral.

CHAPTER 1

Introduction

This book describes a new 21st-century version of high school academic tracking. This modern approach to tracking is far different from the 20th-century model, where "sticky" ability group tracks were laid down for students in the 9th grade that would steer them into the workplace, trade school, the military, or college. Instead, 21st-century American education takes on a new approach: *All* students get ready for college and career, regardless of where they may end up or wish to end up. All students are expected to take high school classes that make them perform at "proficient" or higher in all subjects. All students are supposed to enroll in enough high school credits to get into college. And if they *individually* show interest, all students are offered a chance to enroll in college-preparatory courses that will tout teaching the soft skills of college rigor with the hard benefit of banking credits in high school to reduce students' eventual college tuition costs.

This book will show how this new approach only fully serves nonrural White populations, leaving the majority of students with college-prep opportunities of lesser quality and lower exchange value than their privileged nonrural White peers, often without the other students even realizing they have been shortchanged. Given the small circles of district catchment zones embedded in historically segregated residential patterns in the United States, many students are unaware that the value of their college-prep credential does not exchange for the same value in college as their fellow college classmates. While their nonrural White peers exchange their high school coursework for free college credits, nonprivileged students accumulate student loans to retake courses that they thought would count in college.

When college-preparatory courses fail to adequately prepare students, it is considered a "counterfeit credential" in 21st-century American education. "Counterfeit" means that the college-prep courses fail to provide their students with the benefits they were promised. For example, an AP course cannot earn value as an exchangeable good unless it is externally appraised; most colleges require a passing score on exams for students to earn college credit. Some students are surrounded by informed adults or peers with this information and thus are structurally embedded in a high school context that affords them the opportunities to earn the exchangeable passing exam score for college credit. Most students never get that chance. Those without a well-informed network operate under the false pretense that a college-prep course listed on their transcript is an exchangeable good in and of itself. As a result, many enter college believing they have educational capital to spend, only to find out by comparing to others that their credentials are counterfeit.

This route to counterfeit credentials is a methodical one with several structural turns along the path that reinforce students' final destination. This book will describe the structural conditions that lead most students down the road to counterfeit credentials while allowing a privileged few an alternative path to bona fide credentials that can give them a leg up in their future college plans.

21st-CENTURY EDUCATION POLICY, IN BRIEF

Education in the United States has undergone immense changes in the early years of the 21st century. Starting with No Child Left Behind (NCLB)—a set of standards that met with an initial wave of resistance—accountability has become the new normal. Most of the public accepts the legitimacy of standardized tests and assumes there to be some inherent value in them.[1] Testing is no longer a supplemental measure of student learning, but the central gauge used.

As part of this paradigm shift, NCLB brought achievement gaps and disparities in educational opportunities between students to the forefront, underscoring the impact of differences in gender, race, ethnicity, special needs, and language status on students' educational outcomes. The work of tracing these gaps shined a bright light on the persistent social problem of different educational outcomes for American children based on where they are born, the households they live in, and the communities they reside in (Gamoran, 2007). Despite other flaws, NCLB pushed state and local education agencies to take a hard look at curriculum, teaching qualifications, and the students who are left on the sidelines in the competition to develop their talents, skills, and intellect (Gamoran, 2007).

NCLB's flaws appeared when it forced schools and communities to react to its findings to avoid sanctions. It created a triage approach to educating students to reach minimal achievement benchmarks, ignoring the students who were dispensable as the "less than 5%" subgroup (Booher-Jennings, 2005). Public postings of school test results made these differences in minimal and maximal achievement (below basic, basic, proficient, advanced, in most states' terms) glaringly obvious. To be sure, this public-facing data uncovered the most egregious deficits in the system. However, parents' perception of their children as part of a classroom of learners morphed into an "every parent for their own child's achievement" competition, as exemplified by recent mania around school choice lotteries (Brody, 2018; Dvorak, 2018; Mackel, 2018; Orfield & Frankenberg, 2013).

As NCLB began to highlight systemic disparities, parents demanded to freely move their children to the school of their choice, creating the next wave of educational legislation across the 50 states. Whether open enrollment, public charter, or voucher based, schools began to advertise to this newly created market of parent-customers. "College prep" became the ubiquitous siren call of these market-savvy schools, and it worked (Epple et al., 2016; Zimmer et al., 2009). When parents could not move their kids, they demanded through PTA and PTO organizations that their traditional public school begin to adapt this much-talked-about college-prep curricula (Freidus, 2016; Posey-Maddox, 2012, 2014; Weber, 2010).

Unfortunately, the push for highbrow college-prep courses ran into a persistent issue in non-highbrow locales: a lack of resources. While parents feverishly pushed to grant their children access to college-preparatory courses, schools were still working with the same or sometimes fewer financial resources to prep, hire, train, and retain teachers to teach the demanded college-preparatory material (Keesler et al., 2008). The needed English, math, and science teachers were not in supply to hire, and the money needed to hire these teachers was absent (Mathis, 2005). While parents demanded college prep, schools had to deal with the reality that funds first needed to be spent on buying state-mandated tests to thwart the looming threat of federal funding (read as: Title I) being pulled from the district budget (Mathis, 2005).

Then the Great Recession befell the nation, and educational budgets began to hemorrhage funding, exacerbating the existing resource disparities aggravated by NCLB. Significantly fewer tax dollars were collected, and emergency actions were taken to keep state budgets balanced—a requirement of most state constitutions. Legislatures cut funding across all state agencies, and education was no exception (American Federation of Teachers [AFT], 2018; Leachman et al., 2017). Districts absorbed the shock of the Great Recession while complying with NCLB testing because the threat of withheld federal funds was too risky. As a result, districts faced severe human and material resource shortages (AFT, 2018; Leachman et al., 2017; Sutcher et al., 2016). Infrastructure (including technology) and hiring ended up being the parts of the schools that were not part of the emergency priority lists. Resource triage replaced any consideration of school resource upkeep (AFT, 2018).

In response to the Great Recession, state legislatures prepared for the next economic shock by rearticulating their budgets in ways that further damaged local education. In doing so, many states passed laws to conserve funds for another rainy day. Part of the prevention measures for many states was to pass school infrastructure repairs on to the local communities. Districts were now instructed to hold local referendums to ask their constituency for a bump in property taxes to fund repairs, whereas in the past, districts added their name to the state queue for infrastructure repairs (Minnesota Rural Education & Schufletowski, 2017; Center for Evaluation,

Policy & Research, 2018; Minnesota Rural Education Association, 2017). The move to a volunteer ask-and-vote model further reinforced disparities as poorer districts voted against unaffordable tax increases while wealthy districts could afford the extra monies in exchange for better education for their younger generation (Siegel-Hawley et al., 2018).

Having laid out the history of these educational policies in the first 20 years of this century, this study pushes forward to new ground rather than rehashing the debate on the legislation. Inequities are in motion, and this book shines a spotlight on the new reality that the legislation of the first 20 years of the century has created and propagated. This study seeks to bring to the public ear a 21st-century discourse on inequality in the American K–12 education system so that the public can act to provide children with thriving places to learn and realize their full potential. The punch line of the book has a familiar tone to it: The changes to the U.S. education system continue to sideline some students in certain schools while others have the best quality resources, training, and opportunities to learn.

This study does not assume or pontificate on the intentions of policy-makers—it simply attempts to deal with the consequences of their actions. That is, nowhere in this book will you the reader find out whether it is intentional to "keep those kids down so that my kids can succeed," if a select clique of elites is working to retain the status as to who gets to attend which schools, or if segregated opportunities to learn is an unintended consequence of the waves of educational reforms in the 21st century. There are plenty of excellent theorists across the disciplines that can pontificate on these intentions. The consequences are familiar and the impacts are real, no matter the intention (see Lewis & Diamond, 2015; Tyson, 2011).

This book focuses on the outcomes: the realized consequences of the high school curriculum today, the stratification of students due to their sociodemographic backgrounds of home and community, the racialized attendance patterns of American students, and the known impact this has on children's life opportunities. This allows us to have an honest discussion about these social facts in order to work toward the common good.

INTERLUDE: WORDS, TERMINOLOGY, AND LANGUAGE USE

Words matter. Language shapes social expectations and concepts (Bourdieu & Passeron, 1977). Language is the most powerful signal of who has the power and who is marginalized by those in power (Allen, 2020; Bourdieu & Passeron, 1977). When certain words are attached to people or persons, the consequences can be life-changing, even fatal (Allen, 2020; Freire, 1970).

New terms will be defined as they newly arise in the text, but there are a few terms that need to be defined and described now so that you as the reader do not get distracted from the larger message of the book.

Words describing race and ethnicity are not only challenging and changing, but they are an especially sensitive topic for Americans. There is an irony laid upon this uneasiness since "race" is a social construct created by imperialists (Allen, 2020; James, 2008; Yellow Bird, 1999). Since race is not biologically real, the words we use to describe it change and morph as social attitudes and political considerations change, even in short periods of time (Gibson, 2010). The U.S. census exemplifies this point: It has seldom used the same set of categories from decade to decade for question/s on racial or ethnic identity since its inception in 1790 (Gibson, 2010). The first use of "check all that apply" on the 2000 census evidences the heterogenous ancestry of many Americans (Gibson, 2010; James, 2008). Before 1960, the census enumerator observations imputed racial information for the census rather than the self-identification used today (Gibson, 2010; James, 2008).

Although race is a social construct, "racial identity becomes part of a group's collective identity and its sense of history and culture, but *the group transfigured and imagined in the physical form of skin color is what appears as race*" (Khalfani et al., 2008, p. 88, emphasis in original). The hegemonic power structure embedded in U.S. culture and history as well as in the current social hierarchy dehumanizes experiences of entire groups of people (Stanfield, 2008, p. 271). Since this book is concerned with the question of students' learning experiences, it is imperative to ask whether there are groups of students who share a collective racial identity who do not get equal chances compared to other groups of students because "race is perhaps the most salient representation of inequality in the Western World" (Bonilla-Silva & Zuberi, 2008, p. 11).

To be clear, I am not a scholar of race or ethnicity. I am a scholar of education and sociology. While I may have some credentials that help me understand the complexity of explaining race and ethnicity, I am no expert. I draw on the foremost experts, many of whom are exposed in Zuberi and Bonilla-Silva's touchstone book *White Methods, White Logic: Racism and Methodology* (2008) and Teranishi, Nguyen, Alcantar, and Curammeng's new book *Measuring Race: Why Disaggregating Data Matters for Addressing Educational Inequality*, to determine how to best describe the data and interpret the findings for you as the reader.

When the details of the paragraphs or tables and figures show the data from the Civil Rights Data Collection (CRDC), I use the terms used in that data collection. CRDC data are parent-reported race and ethnic affiliations of their children. When parents skip completing that section of their child's district information sheet, district administrators are instructed to use observational methods to impute race and ethnicity (U.S. Department of Education, 2008). In 2013–14, the following racial and ethnic terminology was used:

- Asian,
- American Indian or Alaska Native,

- Black,
- Hispanic,
- Native Hawaiian or other Pacific Islander,
- Two or more races, and
- White (Sanametrix & American Institutes for Research, 2016).

Importantly, the CRDC technical standards do not allow for students with Hispanic ancestry to choose a racial category (U.S. Department of Education, 2008). As a result, it is important for readers to interpret the other six labels as specifically excluding students who identify as Hispanic. In places like Arizona, there are likely larger reporting errors from children when parents completing their child's intake form need to choose if they opt for a primary identity for their child as solely Hispanic, American Indian, or White; otherwise they could choose two or more races, which could capture American Indian and White, but not the Hispanic ancestry.

Similarly, when I discuss the CRDC data on curriculum, I use "AP" or "IB" to identify it.[2] I use "college prep" or "CP" when I discuss the AP and IB results together and when the implications from the AP and IB results converge on joint implications and conclusions.

When I write about prior research, I use the terms that the scholars used in their writings. "College and career prep" is only used in relation to reviewing prior literature. No conclusions from this project can be assumed to translate into the career-prep realm since no data related to that curriculum is assessed here. In addition, earlier writings about tracking, for example, typically used terms such as "white and black students" rather than the contemporary use of "White, European American" and "African American" students. Many strides have occurred since the 1980s to not ascribe racial terms to students or persons as a static trait or status. Instead, race and ethnicity are now (correctly) understood as identities of persons that change with society's further evolution into understanding the role of heritage and culture on one's own life as well as in relation to the dominant society (Bonilla-Silva, 2019; Khalfani et al., 2008).

When I write about the implications from the analysis or how to look forward into the future of high school opportunities to learn, I use contemporary terms that keep tight to the data results to reduce overgeneralization or confounding of group identity. Thus, I do not use the term "Latinx" in this book because the data asked about students' Hispanic ancestry. While there is overlap of Hispanic and Latinx, one references language heritage (Hispanic) and the other geographical ancestry (Latinx) (MacDonald, 2001). While there is an emerging scholarship on Pan Latinx, it exceeds the data collected by the CRDC. Hispanic also connotes a pan-ethnicity that reclaims politization of colonizers (Zerquera et al., 2020). Moreover, students with ancestry tied to indigenous cultures in the Central and South Americas do not agree on whether or not to identify as Latinx and/or Hispanic in addition to their indigenous ancestry (Zerquera et al., 2020). This tension is somewhat reflected in the specificity in the Chicano movement (Zerquera et al., 2020). While these delineations may seem trivial to some readers, the links to one's history and ancestry are vital, especially among groups of people who experienced centuries of oppression from rulers who tried to abolish their cultural memory (Bonilla-Silva, 2019; Zerquera et al., 2020).

To avoid generalizing too far beyond the reaches of the data, this book discusses larger implications by students who identify as follows:

- Black, non-Hispanic;
- Native Americans;
- Indigenous Peoples to Hawaii and the Pacific Islands;
- Hispanic;
- Multiracial/ethnic;
- Pan-Asian;
- White, non-Hispanic.

If results point to the all students except White, non-Hispanic students, "students of color" will be used.

Admittedly, some contemporary ears are uneasy using Black, non-Hispanic as a term instead of African American, but the choice is not without reason. Since these data did not ask about students' ancestry tied to the Middle Eastern, Indian (subcontinent), or African migrant, it is not possible to decipher if the findings tie to the centuries of enslavement and oppression of students with ancestry central to the African American identity or if the findings are related to skin complexion and the various biases and discrimination associated with it (Asante et al., 2016; Bonilla-Silva, 2019; Griffin & Mwangi, 2020; O'Connor et al., 2007; Zuberi & Bonilla-Silva, 2008). Of course, biases and discrimination intimately intertwine with the American educational system based on a racialized social system of external observations of skin complexion (Allen et al., 2008; Bonilla-Silva, 2019; Hunter, 2007), but the depth of trauma associated with it culturally links to African American communities in very different sociopolitical ways than to Middle Eastern, Indian, or African migrant communities (Asante et al., 2016; Griffin & Mwangi, 2020).

In addition, these data do not distinguish between Asian ancestries. A wide array of literature abounds to explain the multifaceted cultural and historical differences among Asian communities. For example, Hmong families who came to the United States as political refugees from helping American soldiers during the Vietnam War bring memories of oppression much different than Japanese families who came as elites and then were expelled to internment camps during World War II (Allen, 2020; Omi et al., 2020). These data cannot decipher how cultural memories and historical oppression impact students' opportunities to learn. Instead, these results are limited to the scope in which they were collected. For this reason, Pan–Asian American is the term used when discussing implications. This emphasis on the broadness of the term reminds readers that important nuance is absent.

The choice to use Native American is particularly because new research finds students coalesce as peers around a shared identity even though tribal configurations among indigenous cultures in the mainland Americas express frustration with the lack of acknowledgment of distinctive cultural identities and histories (Brady et al., 2020; Shotton, 2020; Tachine et al., 2017).[3] Moreover, Indigenous Peoples to the Pacific vigorously fought for distinction from American Indian nomenclature due to their ethnic independence and historical intersection with European and Asian colonizers (Hafoka et al., 2020).

As the 2020 census reflects, social, political, and cultural nuances also exist among Whites. Although these "shades of White" (Perry, 2002) have exclusionary power within-group and are not mutually exclusive for individual persons, the concept of Whiteness is itself exclusionary (Zuberi & Bonilla-Silva, 2008, p. 40). The U.S. social system materially benefits Whites based on observational characteristics (Bonilla-Silva, 2019), whether an individual passes for White or personally identifies with it (Steers-McCrum, 2018).

A note on capitalization and racial terms: The thinking on capitalization (and hyphenating, for that matter) vacillates. At one point in history, capitalizing words reflecting complexion was considered offensive in that complexion does not define a person as a proper noun (Wachal, 2000). However, changing the lexicon phrasing order that speaks of race as self-identity rather than an imposed status has changed the orientation of referencing terms related to the construct of race. Capitalizing "Black" and "White" instead of using "black" and "white" distinguishes human groups from generic colors (APA, 2020, p. 142). However, the *Publication Manual of the American Psychological Association, 7th Edition* (the style of this publisher) with this same logic does not capitalize "multiracial" (APA, 2020, p. 143). Capitalization of terms related to ethnicity historically remains stable since they are not socially relative constructs but instead proper nouns that describe specific cultural or historical groups, such as Hispanic or Asian (APA, 2020, p. 143).

Lastly, whenever possible, "heritage" or "ancestry" is used whenever the reader is to hold the importance of history in tandem with the meaning in the sentence. "Identity" is used in most other references to general discussions to emphasize the importance of self-identification to claim group affiliation.

As this book ages, the lexicon will continue to evolve, and these writings will likely seem tone-deaf to important nuances not addressed in this narrative.

CONTRIBUTION

This book seeks to identify the factors of variations in quality of college-preparatory curriculum across high schools in the United States, a longstanding gap in education research (Bourdieu & Passeron, 1977; Coleman, 1990). To tackle this gap, the college-prep landscape is viewed through lenses of prior tracking and educational stratification theories. Earlier research needed to rely on the use of grades and course descriptions from administrative transcript records from nationally representative sample-based datasets of National Educational Longitudinal Study (NELS) and Educational Longitudinal Study (ELS); these data have traditionally been the only reliable proxies in the intensely state-based education system in the United States that leaves little room for any type of national assessment of curriculum or its quality.[4] In contrast, this study relies on a first-of-its-kind dataset, the Civil Rights Data Collection (CRDC), a census of Advanced Placement (AP) and International Baccalaureate (IB) curriculum participation in American high schools.

It also provides AP exam pass rates. These exam scores offer a general pass/fail assessment of the quality of the student learnings that take place in AP classrooms across the United States (U.S. Office of Civil Rights, 2017). This pass/fail metric provides a solid threshold to assess whether or not the course fulfilled its promise to students regarding its exchange rate as a college-prep course exchangeable for college credit.

SUMMARY OF CHAPTERS

Chapter 2 describes the central puzzle that motivates this study: How does the rhetoric of "college for all" in U.S. society impact educational stratification in the 21st century? This chapter uses sociological theories to help explain the empirical disconnect between the rising rates of enrolling in college and the stagnating rates of college graduation. These sociological theories outline the role of material and human resources in schools in creating this disconnect. To round out the chapter, four states (Arizona, Florida, Michigan, and North Carolina) are used as case studies throughout the book to exemplify this national problem.

Chapter 3 describes the frame of the puzzle: the high schools where the rhetoric first hits the ground. This chapter explains the variety of districts and charter schools in which high school students study, the students with whom they attend school, and the courses they take. These details help frame how to interpret the clusters of the puzzle that begin to be pieced together in the rest of the book.

Chapter 4 begins to make sense of the puzzle using the foundational aspect of access to opportunity in college-prep courses in high school.

This chapter puts together puzzle pieces to reveal the picture that 10% of American high school students have no AP or IB courses available to them anywhere in their district. Then a close look in this section finds that this 10% disproportionately disenfranchises opportunities for students who attend districts in rural America. This chapter also explains how the trends among charter schools differ from the public districts.

Chapter 5 furthers the puzzle's completion by taking the data on the districts and charter schools that do offer college prep from Chapter 4 and examining which students participate in the AP or IB courses offered versus which students do not. This chapter explains how the different uses of resources promote either greater or lesser equitable participation in these courses. Equitable participation is virtually absent, and inequality is highly racialized. This chapter explains how some districts' disparity arises from hoarding resources within schools to create a college-prep "track" while other districts pile up their resources on a single college-prep "school."

Chapter 6 pushes further toward rounding out the shape of the puzzle by mobilizing the participation data and asks: What is the quality of these courses? A measure of students' mastery of course material describes quality. This chapter investigates why some college-prep courses in some districts and charter schools deliver higher-quality outcomes but not in others. There is a strong clustering in the data that shows that urban schools that serve primarily students of color tend to have poor outcomes because sometimes no schools administer prep exams to their students, or few actually pass those exams if they take them.

Chapter 7 looks at the completed puzzle, showing how each of the clusters of data come together to create a clear picture of the structural issues impacting college prep in U.S. education. From a structural perspective, these questions are answered: What are the inequities and consequences of those inequities for American high school students? How do districts and charter schools sustain educational attainment gaps that disenfranchise entire groups of students while advantaging other groups?

Chapter 8 moves beyond the completed puzzle to consider the implications of colleges ceasing to exchange any college-prep capital if they begin to feel defrauded by the unpredictable quality of college-prep high school coursework. This chapter describes schools and districts in the data that equitably deliver quality college-prep coursework to their high schoolers in an effort to set forth educational policy suggestions for departments of education as well as district administrators about how to raise the equitable quality of these courses to thwart this looming problem. Also discussed is how to restore trust with families who may feel betrayed by the broken social compact regarding the promise of college readiness for all students.

CHAPTER 2

A Simmering Problem

with Kristi Donaldson

This chapter starts assembling the corner pieces to the puzzle—in the United States, educational opportunities shape life outcomes. Research clearly shows the widening advantages afforded to Americans with college degrees: higher income, greater wealth, less unemployment, less obesity, healthier births, longer life expectancies, greater job satisfaction, and even less likelihood to divorce than Americans without a four-year degree (Ma et al., 2016; Wang, 2015).

In the last 20 years, the financial and health benefits associated with holding a college degree have strengthened while those same markers have weakened, or at best remained unchanged, for those holding less than a college degree (Ma et al., 2016; Wang, 2015). Economists typically explain this trend as a market response to the rise of technology in work: Jobs not requiring a college education (with the exception of the trades) are growing more prone to automation and thus are less stable and more vulnerable to layoffs. In contrast, those jobs that do require a college education tend to be the ones designing and running the same automation-reducing, non-degree jobs or fall into the category of service positions that are not easily automated. This difference between job stability and the constant threat of layoffs is proposed as the driving force behind the growing gap in financial and health differences by educational attainment.

For example, economic reports out of Georgetown show that post–Great Recession, those with college degrees gained the most jobs (about 73%) during the recovery (Carnevale et al., 2016), while those with a high school degree or less education experienced no job recovery. Furthermore, the re-employment of workers with less than a high school degree occurred in the significantly lower paid and less stable service and hospitality industries. In this postrecession world, nearly 75% of the 30 fastest-growing occupations typically need a certificate, associate degree, or higher education for entry (U.S. Bureau of Labor Statistics, 2017). Figure 2.1 illustrates this volatility of the workforce pre—and post–Great Recession.

The benefits of having a college degree are not lost on policymakers. The modification of state graduation requirements to align with college

Figure 2.1. Job Instability over 10 Years by Educational Attainment

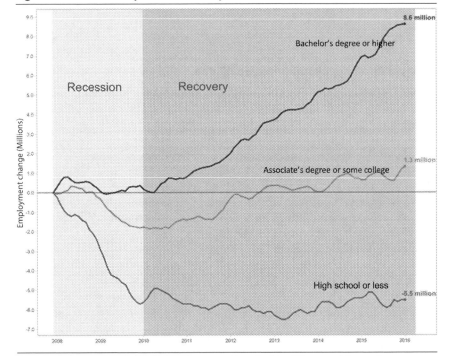

Note: Employment includes all workers age 18 and older. The monthly employment numbers are seasonally adjusted using the U.S. Census Bureau x-12 procedure and smoothed using a 4-month moving average.

Source: Georgetown University Center on Education and Workforce analysis of *Current Population Survey* (CPS) data: 2007–2018.

admissions standards shows state legislatures' desire and demand for students to graduate high school "ready for college and career." However, the post–high school "career-ready" portion of this goal is seldom anything other than a tagline. For example, in Michigan, where a high school education used to support a solidly middle-class career and lifestyle, the new 2015 standards for graduation align the admissions minimums to Michigan's state universities: 4 years of math and English/language arts, 3 years of science and social studies, and (phasing in) 2 years of world language (Michigan Department of Education, 2017). Standards to "career ready" is left undefined in Michigan and thus is assumed to equate to these college readiness standards.

To begin the work of laying out the puzzle regarding college prep, you the reader are asked to remember that all the educational issues being discussed affect the trajectory of each student's future and quality of life. The rest of this chapter works to explain the rise of "college for all" and "college readiness" standards across the United States that aim to prepare young people for 21st-century adulthood. Theories presented anticipate the social responses from these educational policies and the associated empirical research that undergird these theories.

Following these discussions, the methods outline how to test the questions about how AP and IB college-prep curricula contribute to these changes and further educational inequality. Yes, further it, not reduce it. The chapters end with illustrations of how this looks among the four "spotlight states" cases of Arizona, Florida, Michigan, and North Carolina.

COLLEGE AND CAREER READINESS = COLLEGE FOR ALL

The idea that a high school education prepared students to become informed citizens—some students via career and others via college—became passé as a 20th-century ideal. Instead, the citizenry aim of the high school education morphed into penalty-avoidance actions to raise achievement test scores (Goldrick-Rab & Mazzeo, 2005; Ravitch, 2010). The move to accountability under NCLB combined with the threat of sanctions pushed districts and schools to focus their energies on increasing the subject knowledge learned to improve students' test scores (Grodsky et al., 2008; Perna & Thomas, 2009; Ravitch, 2010). Although test score infatuation was not the intent of NCLB, it became the reality (Ravitch, 2010).

Academic curriculum in high school shifted as testing became more and more important. Knowledge in math, English, and science that could be easily tested to find gaps and assess knowledge levels became simple measures to use to compare school quality. The growth of students' socio-emotional skills needed to be a day care attendant or the teamwork skills needed to serve in the military were not exactly in the scope of the achievement gaps that NCLB was aiming to reduce, and these skills were almost impossible to measure on a standardized state test. Unsurprisingly, the academic curricula associated with more testable subjects ended up being adopted rather than more abstract skills in the creation of a one-size-fits-all (Barnes & Slate, 2013) curriculum in high school to meet the NCLB educational policy demands (Ravitch, 2010).

All of these changes were not without some benefit to students where good curricula were sorely missing. It did make some things better. But it really only touched on the shoddiest of the shoddiest curricula where kids didn't have teachers certified in the subject area being taught (Dee & Jacob, 2010). (Do you remember when you were a kid when you had your gym teacher one year teaching you English? That kind of thing is less likely to happen since NCLB.)

What this book will show, however, is that since the "college for all" curriculum became the mandated high school graduation requirements, the quality of these curricula became more opaque. States raised high school graduation requirements, standards were revised, but *quality* went unregulated. One might wonder, how did all districts in the whole United States in only a few years suddenly have adequate human resource teaching power to teach physics in nearly every high school? The short answer is they didn't. For example, a 2008 report about Michigan estimated that 25% of schools were undersupplied to meet their math requirements, with half of these schools also undersupplied in English teachers (Keesler et al., 2008). The long answer is found in the following chapters as the puzzle pieces come together to show how these shortages of human and material resources drive the vastly different quality of curricula across the country. This disparity in quality becomes glaringly transparent when students enter college and find themselves facing additional years there, failing to graduate, and/or possessing fewer career-ready citizenry skills that were de-prioritized since NCLB policy changes (Rosenbaum, 2001; Schneider & Stevenson, 1999).

The de-prioritizing of career readiness in high school additionally creates a problem of leaving U.S. employers in a Hobbesian world where employers no longer trust that a high school diploma has prepared a worker for the workplace (Rosenbaum, 2001). As Rosenbaum discusses, employers now bypass the diploma as a guide and make use of informal networks and signals to judge the fit of an applicant during the application and interview for a job position. This approach ends up creating secondary issues such as homogeneity and discriminatory behaviors in hiring (Rosenbaum, 2001).

Research clearly shows that the "college for all" curriculum standard has unintended consequences for children's lifelong opportunities. Nonetheless, that standard is perpetuated through public rhetoric as exemplified by President Obama's 2016 State of the Union Address speaking to "mak[ing] college affordable for every American" and by the Lumina Foundation's 2025 postsecondary goal of 60% of Americans having high-quality degrees, certificates, and credentials by 2025 (Merisotis, 2017). Lumina has even provided funding to more than 60 cities and communities across the nation, with each community having its own postsecondary attainment goal and strategy (e.g., Newark with "25 by 2025," Cleveland with "65 by 2025," etc.) (Lumina Foundation, 2020).

FROM HIGH SCHOOL "COLLEGE FOR ALL" EXPECTATION TO ACTUALLY GOING TO COLLEGE

In addition to the political reasons for the rise of "college for all," there is the practical question of whether or not these new 21st-century policies have actually improved college readiness. For example, has the "college for all" expectation improved college attendance? Research by Attewell and

Domina clearly shows that raising the curricular intensity of students' high school schedules in the early 1990s does increase the odds that they will enter college (Attewell & Domina, 2008). Since then, we continue to see a modest rise in college enrollment since 2000, from 63% to 70%.[1] Figure 2.2 shows that the 7-percentage-point increase is not across all students, however. The increase in enrollment is primarily driven by the 24-percentage-point enrollment increase among Hispanic students. College enrollment for this student subgroup has risen at a rapid pace and is now on par with White, non-Hispanic students' college enrollment. The White, non-Hispanic and Black, non-Hispanic rates, in contrast, have been virtually flat, while Pan-Asian students' rate has inched upwards. Figure 2.3 shows rises primarily associated with greater enrollment among students from lower-income households.

When we look at enrolled college students' home locale in Figure 2.4, a rise of 5–6 percentage points in college enrollment occurs among all students

Figure 2.2. Enrollment Trends in Two- and Four-Year Colleges by Racial and Ethnic Identity of Enrolling Students

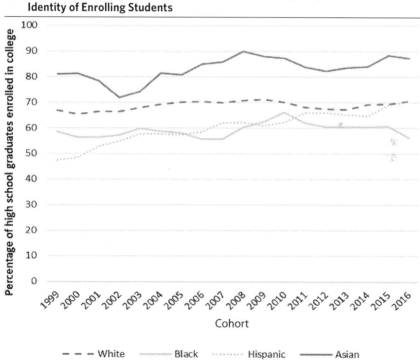

Note: Three-year moving average reported.

Source: Table 302.20, Digest of Education Statistics. https://nces.ed.gov/programs/digest/d17/tables/dt17_302.20.asp

Figure 2.3. Enrollment Trends in Two- and Four-Year Colleges by Parents' Income of Enrolling Students

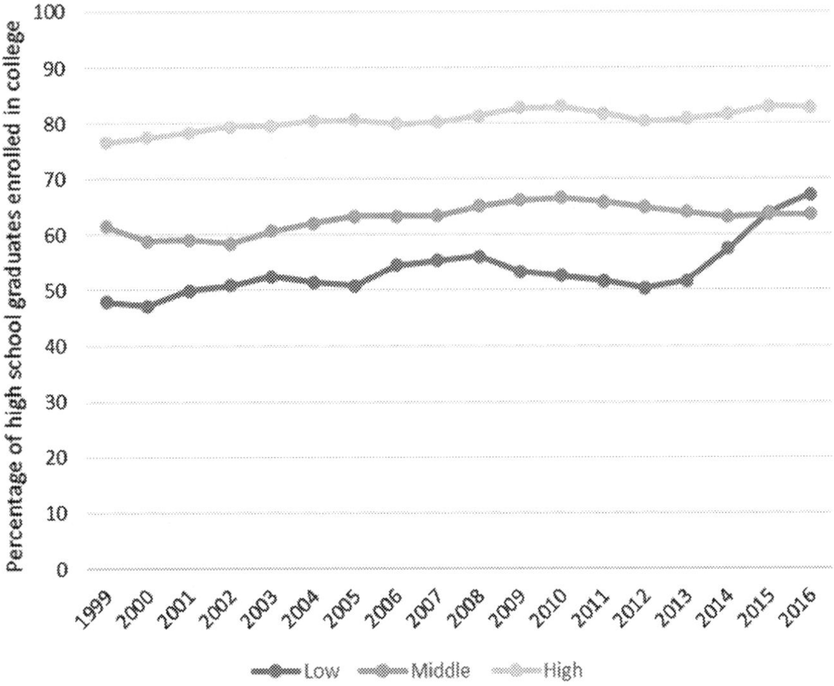

Note: Three-year moving average reported.

Source: Table 302.30, *Digest of Education Statistics*. https://nces.ed.gov/programs/digest/d17/tables/dt17_302.30.asp

except suburban students, who remain relatively flat. These yearly trends keep steady the gap by community locale. Although these gaps appear small on a 0–100 scale, a seven-point gap is a 20% difference in attending college between students attending township schools versus suburban schools. As Chapter 4 will show, locale continues as a major stratifier when it comes to access to college-prep coursework.

When we look at college graduation from those enrolled, a similarly slight uptick occurs in earning the bachelor's degree credential (Figure 2.5). A 7-percentage-point gain in four-year graduation rates occurs from 34% to 41% of enrolled students. In the 1990s, Domina and Saldana also found a modest increased likelihood to graduate college associated with a boost in curricular intensity (Domina & Saldana, 2012). But this completion rate change pales in comparison to the college enrollment changes.

Since 2000, racialized gaps in college graduation persist. White, non-Hispanic and Hispanic students tow the average rate, while Pan-Asian

Figure 2.4. Enrollment Trends in Two- and Four-Year Colleges by School Locale of Enrolling Students

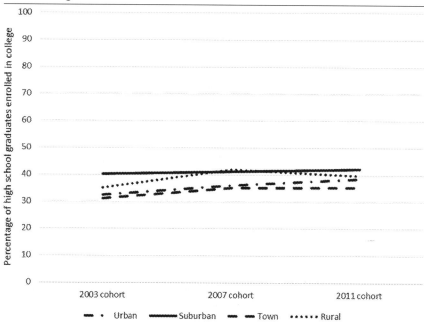

Source: Table 302.40, *Digest of Education Statistics.* https://nces.ed.gov/programs/digest/d16/tables/dt16_302.40.asp

students are the first group to hit the 50% mark for four-year graduation. Black, non-Hispanic students' graduation remained completely flat and the lowest of all student subgroups. Clearly, disparities exist when college graduation rates are compared to those who initially enrolled in college. But the gaps are nearly the same since all subgroups moved up at the same rate. The exception to this trend is the flatness of Black, non-Hispanic college graduation rates, which means that the gap between Black, non-Hispanic and all other students has widened in the past decade of college graduates.

Considering these persistent gaps in college enrollment and college graduation, the social issue raised by theorists has real teeth: What happens when the high school curricula are geared to "college for all" when the majority of students will not earn a college diploma? How does the quality of their high school education become critical to shaping the opportunities of students? The next section describes the puzzle of the variation in quality of the college-prep curriculum and its impact on American young people.

Figure 2.5. Bachelor's Degree Graduation Trends by Racial and Ethnic Identity of Enrolled Students

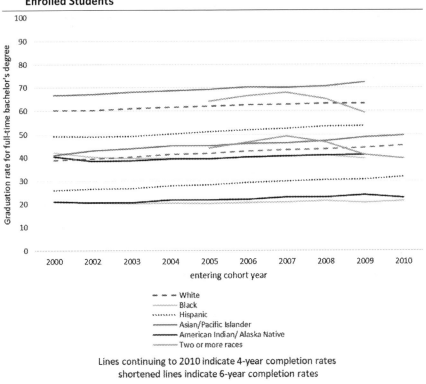

Lines continuing to 2010 indicate 4-year completion rates
shortened lines indicate 6-year completion rates

Source: Table 326.10, *Digest of Education Statistics.* https://nces.ed.gov/programs/digest
/d17/tables/dt17_326.10.asp

THE PUZZLE

As just reviewed, the path to college has widened. With the new education policies of the 21st century, a college education is no longer reserved for society's intellectual elite and is available to most everyone in the United States. A high school diploma (including its equivalent) is all that is required to begin the college experience, and fully 84% of high school students today earn this required high school credential (McFarland et al., 2018).

College-preparatory classes in high school, like Advanced Placement (AP) and International Baccalaureate (IB), have similarly democratized and are widely available to more than just the highest-achieving students (Attewell & Domina, 2008; College Board, 2018; Donaldson, 2017). These courses, in particular, can bolster students' exposure to the subject matter and critical-thinking skills that influence the *quality* of their college application components to distinguish them from other applicants (Attewell & Domina, 2008; Domina & Saldana, 2012; Donaldson, 2017; Smith et al., 2017). Colleges look to students' transcript grades and exam scores in these courses to assess applicants' effort and success in these courses to gauge the likelihood of their success during college and to graduate (Smith et al., 2017). These student-level differences in college preparation help sort students into which colleges they attend and graduate, as well as how they eventually impact lifetime earnings, health, and happiness (Ma et al., 2016; Smith et al., 2017; Wang, 2015).

Though more students experience college preparation than ever before, these learning opportunities vary substantially. Readying for college during high school is structured differently across the United States and depends on the school a student attends. Some schools offer advanced college-prep courses, others do not. Some schools are effective at teaching such courses, others are not. What is common is that students do not have control over these meso-level structures. Many students and their families take the rhetoric of "college for all" at face value, trusting that their school system is upholding the social compact of college readiness.

With college prep, the *quality* of these courses varies widely and demonstrates that course titles or enrollment numbers do not indicate whether or not the course fulfilled the promise of readying students for college. As an example, in the space of one Michigan county, 9 of its 10 districts enroll hundreds of AP course seats, yet some of these districts pass fewer than 5% of their AP students on any AP exam. This failure to deliver on a quality college-prep experience in high school is a failure of educational policy. It leaves students with counterfeit credentials, where they cannot exchange this educational good for college course credit. The expected benefits of the college-prep course never materialize to buy what it promised.

The bottom line is that the rhetoric and energy around "college for all" in high school do not bear out in college enrollment and completion. Today's ratio of college completers suggests that when employers look to hire a college-educated workforce, they see much the same pool of candidates that they saw 20 years ago; it's just a slightly larger pool now. This means that the kids who have been historically sidelined in education appear to now just be sidelined at a later stage in their educational trajectory (Rosenbaum, 2001).

The puzzle put together in this study explains how this happens. The study asks: If states are improving their high school curricula and raising high school graduation standards, why does this K–12 policy change not convert into college completion? Do "college for all" and "college ready" mean the same thing across U.S. high school settings? Does the value of college-prep coursework from different high schools exchange at the same rate in the college marketplace? The upcoming chapters provide these answers to piece together the puzzle of continued disenfranchisement of historically marginalized students amidst the newly uniform "college for all" high school educational policies across the United States.

THEORETICAL FRAMEWORK

Sociology offers some theories to imagine how and why these patterns in college-preparation outcomes occur. Theories explain that once an educational level, like high school completion, approaches saturation, its value decreases; it no longer provides the same distinct credential or advantage as it once did. The minimum amount of education needed for economic participation or to earn a "good job" (i.e., a middle-class income) also increases. Today, a high school diploma will no longer suffice, as about 75% of the fastest-growing occupations typically need some postsecondary credential (U.S. Bureau of Labor Statistics, 2017).

AP, IB, and other advanced courses provide a means by which individuals can *qualitatively* distinguish themselves from others with a high school diploma. This is best illustrated with Lucas's theory of effectively maintained inequality (EMI), which proposes that horizontal, or qualitative, stratification surfaces once particular educational levels near saturation (Lucas, 2001). This is different from maximally maintained inequality (MMI), which posits that when educational levels approach saturation, inequality at that level will decrease (Raftery & Hout, 1993). The distinction between MMI and EMI here is that although the educational level—high school graduation—approaches saturation where the majority of adults have the degree qualitative differences remain in the type of high school education received (EMI).

The lack of quality assurance in college-prep courses especially impacts students and parents with little cultural capital for the college admissions process (Cipollone & Stich, 2017; Eaton, 2001; Kilgore, 1991; Lareau, 2000; Oakes & Guiton, 1995; Yosso, 2005). These students and parents hear the promise that children who take an AP course can earn college credit and expect that to bear out. This message is often framed as a cost-saving benefit: Students will have to pay for fewer credits once they get to college, reducing their time to degree and increasing their likelihood of graduating (Evans, 2019). For students and parents with less college savvy, this message omits the process by which this credential gets validated. It is not just about taking the college-prep course, but earning a passing score on the external exam that converts the high school course good into legitimate exchangeable capital for college credit (Evans, 2019). It is not enough for students to simply to enroll in AP or IB courses at their school; they must also pass their end-of-year AP or IB exams (Evans, 2019). These students and parents with little cultural capital regarding this process (Cipollone & Stich, 2017; Eaton, 2001; Kilgore, 1991; Lareau, 2000; Oakes & Guiton, 1995; Yosso,

2005) will not know their college-prep capital is counterfeit until they go to exchange it at college without an accompanying passing test score.

In a stark contrast, students who have higher cultural capital or access to it are fully aware of the operational procedures in admissions requiring that they pass the external exam in order to earn the associated college credit. These students come equipped with this knowledge via their parents, their friends, or perhaps even guidance counselor advocates (Cipollone, & Stich, 2017; Deil-Amen & Tevis, 2010; Kelly, 2004; Kilgore, 1991; Klugman, 2012; Lareau, 2015; Lewis & Diamond, 2015; Ndura et al., 2003; Witenko et al., 2017). These more knowledgeable students also know that postsecondary institutions do not use transcript grades to assign college credit upon admission.

This gap in knowledge that a passing exam score is necessary to earn college credit operates as a stratifying agent. Students surrounded by informed adults or peers have a chance to earn an exchangeable good for college credit, but those without the knowledge operate under a false pretense that an AP or IB course listed on their transcript is an exchangeable good in and of itself. These courses cannot earn value as an exchangeable good unless a student's accumulated knowledge from the course is externally appraised. Until there is an external auditor (e.g., College Board score on an AP exam or IB diploma or subject-specific content exam), the course has little value. Some students assume their transcript course will transfer to earned college credit, and it is not until they enroll in college that they discover that their college-prep course in and of itself has no exchangeable value for college credit, hence it is counterfeit (Cipollone & Stich, 2017; College Board, 2018). Moreover, if a given course is not rigorous enough and fails to prepare the students for the exam, then any cultural capital knowledge of the passing score information becomes moot. For those students admitted to more selective colleges based on their course transcripts but with no exam score, it may seem that they did exchange their college-prep capital for the selective college admission good, but the failure to test the quality of the course likely signals inferior course rigor, which will manifest in counterfeit college readiness skills when they begin their college coursework. Thus, these ill-equipped students will not recognize they were sold a counterfeit good in high school until they enter the college classroom.

Students who enroll in college-prep courses have some advantages over those who do not. Taking (and passing, high school grade wise) college-prep courses can benefit students during college admissions, as colleges often look to see if students have maximized their course-taking opportunities in high school. Yet colleges do not use transcript grades to assign college credit on admission. At colleges that offer credit for advanced coursework, students can only earn credit by passing their AP exam(s).

Similar to the expansion of mass education (Collins, 1979), "college for all" via college-ready goals appears to provide for a more equitable and meritocratic system. Most of the growth occurs at the bottom end of the educational distribution to "raise the floor" to increase the minimum threshold. Those at the top still maintain distinct advantages, such as through real, authentic advanced coursework at the high school level (Domina & Saldana, 2012; Domina et al., 2015; Penner et al., 2015). This study will show how the push for college-ready coursework has simply "reproduced that [sociodemographic] hierarchy at a more advanced level" (Domina & Saldana, 2012, p. 703).

Indeed, the data trends on high school graduation and college enrollment support an increasing average proposed by Attewell and Domina (2008), but these changes are not translating into similarly sized boost in college graduation. To explain this disconnect, the effectively maintained inequality (EMI) theory (Lucas, 1999) describes how quality becomes the differentiator when something like college-bound résumés of high school students become ubiquitous. EMI explains that if the *access* part of a resource holds nearly ubiquitous in a system and no longer creates differences, then the *quality* aspect of the resource will be used as the stratifying device. Thus, EMI would shape a hypothesis that if high school seniors' applications to college all list the same baseline transcript courses, then it will be the quality of the courses, identified by titles such as AP and IB as well as the indicators of content mastery via the scores on AP exams or IB diplomas, that will together signal the quality of the acquisition of college readiness during their high school education.

When we look to explain the differences of quality between courses, let's start at the foundation: resources. Coleman (1990) explains there is a diseconomy of resources with a two-part sequence: how resources are dispersed to schools and how students receive them (new or tattered, accredited or not, etc.). This syncs well with the argument that the schools' resources are only as good as the teachers and their professional skills in how to use the resources (Gamoran et al., 2000; Domina et al., 2017). And yet there is a basic foundation of material resources teachers need in order to put their skills to work (Fahle & Reardon, 2017). As such, the diseconomy of resources idea can be operationalized as districts' resource dispersal to schools (material resources) and teachers' skills in using the resources (human resources). Although a resource argument can seem pedestrian, the economic gaps across U.S. communities starkly define differences in student achievement, growth, and opportunities to learn (Fahle & Reardon, 2017).

The remainder of the book addresses how the human and material resource differences between school districts condition the actualized differences in quality of "college for all" across the diverse U.S. high school population. Particular attention is paid to the disparities around certain groups of students who attend districts with and without these human and material resources.

METHODS

This study focuses on districts because they are the ground-floor level where resources are delivered by the state before being sorted and distributed to schools. Once districts receive funds, they distribute them to their schools and provide parameters on how to spend the resources. The human and material resources in schools are used in consultation with districts and constrained by the community economy.

Figure 2.6 shows the working hypotheses guiding this study regarding the interaction of material and human resources within the context of community economies. Districts with few material (i.e., money) and human (i.e., appropriately certified teachers) resources will be unable to provide college-prep opportunities to their students. Districts rich in material and human resources will be able to provide quality, externally verified (i.e., passing scores on exams) college-prep opportunities to their students. Districts with some material resources with human resources spread across many schools will likely be unable to deliver high-quality college-prep opportunities, but districts with similar material resources that concentrate human resources in some of their schools but not others will produce a

Figure 2.6. Hypotheses of District Resources on College Prep Curriculum Quality

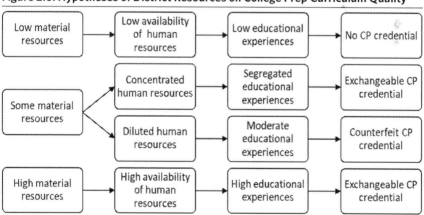

Measures

Material resources = financial means of a district community

Human resources = teachers qualified and available to teach college prep

CP credential = value of high school college-prep curriculum for college

bifurcation of high quality in some of its schools and no opportunities in its other schools.

AP and IB Coursework as the Ideal Curricula to Discuss "College for All" Impact

Where do AP and IB fit in the "college for all" story? "College for all" discussions typically focus on students who might not otherwise go to college. The implied idea is that all students, regardless of background, educational preparation, and so forth, can and should go to college. After all, students most likely to take advanced coursework are those likely to attend college. So why do these courses make for an ideal measure to use in this study? Unlike other curricula, these courses are nationally recognized and monitored by agencies external to the local, state, or federal education agencies. The courses, therefore, provide an apolitical, legislative-free avenue to map patterns of inequalities in the move toward college-ready high school graduation standards.

This study uses the Civil Rights Data Collection (CRDC), a mandated federal collection of curricula data by the U.S. Department of Education. As such, there is no selective opt-out of districts, and there is no state-level intervention on the data collection. The districts and charter schools directly report their data to the federal government on the AP and IB course enrollments and test-taking to represent the college-preparatory curriculum (U.S. Office of Civil Rights, 2017). The CRDC is a *census* of college-preparation curriculum data from all traditional and charter public schools in the United States. The enrollment data therefore allow us to see where and who has access and exposure to such college-prep coursework. The pass/fail rates provide a measure of the quality of the courses: whether or not the prep course fulfilled its promise of an exchangeable educational good with college value.

Empirically, this study excludes the dual enrollment coursework collected by the CRDC in the analyses. Dual enrollment data include students' course-taking in everything from mechanics at the local trade school to organic chemistry at the local four-year college. Since this study regards college prep exclusively, the inability to disaggregate college from career-prep courses in dual enrollment[2] induces error and so it is not included.

Of course, some students are expected to pass and some to fail due to their effort matched to the rigor of the course ("opportunity to learn" in the classic Sørenson and Hallinan [1977] idea). However, when entire schools of students fail to pass their exams, that is no longer individual and can be no less than a meso-level structural issue.

These meso-level phenomena are coined "counterfeit" when entire groups of students find themselves in schools without access to, participation in, or passing their exams because "counterfeit" encapsulates how students are unaware that the product they receive is a mock version of the real thing. It is only once they reach college where they find out that they do not earn college credit or, even more insulting, need to take remedial courses to get ready for the rigor of college courses. It is not until they leave the high school marketplace that they find out that the educational good they worked to earn is of inferior quality, only posing as the real learning experience. As a result, these students end up paying more for college than they anticipated.

As the book progresses, the statistical methods used to test the hypotheses will be described. For those interested, the online appendices are filled with the tabular output of the statistical models.

Assumptions

There are several assumptions that underlie this study. It assumes that students are equally able to learn no matter their ascribed, cultural, or zip code backgrounds. It assumes that there is a social obligation to uphold the promise in the American educational system of a free and fair education to all students. It assumes that school systems are responsible for delivering equal educational opportunities to any student in their purview. This section describes how to methodologically attend to these ideological assumptions in order to reach empirically sound conclusions.

Districts commonly work collaboratively with their schools to determine priorities. To check this idea, this study includes charter schools in the analysis to test if districts act as a structural constraint on school resource use. Spoiler alert: They don't. Charter schools react to human and material resource constraints in much the same way as schools under district control.[3] There is no significant "charter school effect" that shows they can better obtain, allocate, and use their resources without district oversight. It does mean that, on average, resource needs impact the execution of "college for all" similarly, no matter the level of state or district regulation.

This study does assume the district student population reflects the community economy. If a district is predominantly serving students experiencing poverty (as identified if all the district schools receive Title I funding), then the associated community is deemed low-income.[4] Community resources are important in light of the impact of referendum ideas discussed a few pages earlier.

This study also takes into account the argument that could be made that material and human resources would be misappropriated on students who are not academically ready for AP or IB. This could be due to academic underperformance and/or that students did not or could not enroll in appropriate course options in middle school to qualify them for AP or IB high school curriculum.

Regarding the latter concern, middle school sequencing really only affects taking calculus college-prep courses since English, history, science, psychology, and other AP or IB courses can stand independent of middle school sequences. Even so, students could, in theory, double up in Algebra I or II in high school with geometry to get to calculus in high school even if they did not get algebra in 8th grade. However, this book addresses this counterargument in Chapter 3 by describing districts with and without AP Calculus and explains why the results are not sensitive to this structural barrier of middle school course sequencing.

Regarding the former concern of ability levels of students, the premise is a deficit position that is widely rejected. However, the analysis will not shy away from testing it head-on. Theoretically, the argument rests on the premise that it can be the case that no students are "above the average" ability in the whole district. The nationally compiled Stanford Education Data Archives (SEDA) data allows a direct test of this premise because it can empirically test the extent to which district achievement relates to offering college prep and how this threshold varies not on an absolute scale of academic abilities but rather one linked to locale and state of residence. This ability argument only holds for the first two parts along the college-prep pipeline (access and participation). For the latter chapter 6, on taking or passing the external exams, this ability theory should not apply since the district did find it reasonable to offer the college-prep courses no matter the students' tested ability levels. That is, if a district does enroll students in college-prep courses and not one student takes or passes the exam, it points to organizational failure to meet the coursework preparedness needs of the enrolled students.

CASE STUDIES: FOUR "SPOTLIGHT STATES"

As ways to illustrate how differences look and act in different parts of the United States, this book uses four states as case studies to illustrate the statistical findings presented. Arizona, Florida, Michigan, and North Carolina well represent the variety and span of state policies shaping student learning. Tables 2.1 and 2.2 summarize the economic similarities and differences among the four case study states. Table 2.1 shows the economics of state spending on education in relation to national norms, while Table 2.2 shows the educational financing sources. These four states have a range of education spending and allocations in relation to the range of household wealth in the state.

In addition to economic issues, educational politics also matters in these case study states. For example, Arizona has been in the news for a variety of education issues related to underserving their students. As Table 2.1 shows, Arizona is the most disparate demographically between teachers and students compared to its policymakers. The highest number of Native American students reside in Arizona (DeVoe & Darling-Churchill, 2008). Arizona

Table 2.1. Descriptions of Education Landscape in Four Spotlight States

State	Proportion of state budget to K–12 education spending	Median income distribution across counties	Teacher Workforce	Education policy and politics
			Average salary, changes in salary since 2000 (in constant dollars); % teachers with <3 yrs experience, union strength/ rank, teacher marches	
AZ	18%	Low-to-average	$47,218; 8% decrease; 16.4%; weakest/51st; statewide protest 2018	Rapidly growing disparity between students and voting population
FL	19%	Wide range of low-to-high	$49,199; 5% decrease; no data; weakest/50th; statewide "walk-in" 2019	Highest concentration of IB; early statewide endorsement of IB as program
MI	27%	Average	$62,028; 10% decrease; 7.3%; strong/16th; Detroit "sickout" 2016	New graduation requirements stress college requirements for HS graduation
NC	22%	Wide range of low-to-high	$47,941; 8.4%; weak/40th; statewide walkout 2018 & 2019	Historical de/segregation

Sources: Noss, A. (2014). "Household Income: 2013," in *American Community Survey Briefs*, edited by U.S. Department of Commerce. Washington, DC: U.S. Census Bureau. *Digest of Education Statistics* (2017), Table 211.60; 209.30.

districts also serve a large concentration of bilingual students, which couples with its narrowly defined English-language learner policies that push most learners out of services prematurely (U.S. Department of Justice Civil Rights Division [USDOJ], 2016). Arizona has experienced years of hard times in recruiting and retaining teachers, especially to serve their English-language learner student population. The abysmal teacher salaries and a trend in decreasing pay do little to help the state recruit and retain teachers. Publicly, teachers have protested their poor working conditions and underfunded classrooms (Flaherty, 2018).

Florida is IB ground zero with an active legislature pushing high-school-to-college transition policies. Like Arizona, it too has low teacher salaries, but there is a wider variety of living expenses depending on where one lives in the state. It is unlawful for teachers to protest or walk off the job in Florida, so they have instead staged "walk-ins" to voice their frustration with education policies in the state (Comparative and International Education Society [CIES], 2019).

Arizona and Florida are also both highly imbalanced between the household ages of voters (retired) who do not have kids in the schools to which they pay their tax dollars.

Michigan is the home state of the U.S. secretary of education Betsy DeVos under the 45th President of the United States, and we know that she was very hands-on in lobbying for legislative changes in her state's policies, including the implementation of the mandatory college-prep curriculum for Michigan graduation (Barrett, 2016). Moreover, it was prosecutors from Michigan who brought the *Milliken v. Bradley* case to the U.S. Supreme Court in 1974 (Chermerinsky, 2002; Clotfelter, 2004). It was this case that halted cross-district integration efforts and codified district boundaries as lines where *Brown v. Board* did not legally cross (Chermerinsky, 2002; Clotfelter, 2004).

The economy changes in the 21st century have also deeply reconfigured the Michigan workforce, as Table 2.1 shows. Given its workforce history, teacher unions in Michigan are considerably strong. Although teachers have experienced a rapid decrease in overall pay during the postrecession time, Michigan teachers' average pay is still solidly a middle-class income.

North Carolina represents the gerrymandered and historically de jure segregated districts where the history of explicit unequal education has deep roots and pervasive generational norms of influence. North Carolina also has one of the most active state education departments in the United States. Although unions are weak in North Carolina and its public employee teachers are prohibited to strike or collectively bargain (§ 95–98.1, 1988), teachers walked out two years in a row to voice their grievances with the politics of education policies (CIES, 2019).

Among the spotlight states, spending varies. Table 2.2 shows that Arizona spends the least amount of money per pupil, which partially reflects a swath of quite economically depressed areas across the state, including vast rural and remote communities. Florida spends the next-lowest amount of per-pupil spending. For both Arizona and Florida, nearly half of the per-pupil funding comes from local sources, which means that local revenue taxes and referendum results can swing amounts per pupil quite widely between districts. Since Florida is on a countywide district mapping, the impact of local revenue is less unequal than in Arizona.

Michigan spends a bit more than average compared to other states per pupil, which is common across upper-Midwest states (Chingos & Blagg, 2017). Michigan's local/state/federal distribution ratio is about the same as North Carolina's; however, the small boundaries in Michigan districts induce a wide range of poverty to affluence concentrated in districts unlike the large countywide district boundaries in North Carolina. Michigan's local income tax laws and higher proportion of state revenue spending on education thus boost the total dollars per student compared to North Carolina. Despite countywide desegregation districts in North Carolina, there still exist a wide range of average household incomes between the counties with the major universities and the rural counties (Glander, 2015).[5]

Table 2.2 also lists the changes in education funding since the turn of the century when NCLB saddled school districts with the costs of annual testing. It also shows how funding allocations responded to the Great

Table 2.2. Descriptions of Education Spending in Four Spotlight States: 2014 Spending and Changes Since 2000 in Spending Ratio for Students with Economic Needs

State	Per-pupil spending and rank (per state income)	Local funds	State funds	Federal funds	Overall funding allocation
AZ	$7,528; 49th	48% PP$; $4,603; steadily regressive ~0.90	38% PP$; $3,543; steadily progressive ~1.07	13% PP$; $1,291; decreasingly progressive from 1.83 to 1.37	Decreasingly progressive
FL	$8,755; 50th	48% PP$; $5,047; steadily equitable ~1.0	40% PP$; $4,265; steadily equitable ~1.02	12% PP$; $1,267; steadily equitable ~1.04	Steadily equitable
MI	$11,110; 23rd	33% PP$; $4,349; regressive to equitable from 0.84 to 0.98	58% PP$; $7,735; steadily equitable ~1.01	9% PP$; $872; increasingly progressive from 1.65 to 1.80	No longer regressive
NC	$8,512; 46th	30% PP$; $3,010; steadily, mildly regressive ~0.95	58% PP$; $5,897; steadily, mildly progressive ~1.04	11% PP$; $1,155; steadily progressive ~1.11	Steadily mixed

Sources: Per-pupil spending (PP$), Table 5, 8, and 11. U.S. Census Bureau, *Public Education Finances: 2014.* (2016). https://www.census.gov/content/dam/Census/library/publications/2016/econ/g14-aspef.pdf; Chingos, M. and K. Blagg. 2017. "How Has Education Funding Changed Over Time?" Washington, DC: Urban Institute, https://apps.urban.org/features/education-funding-trends/; Dollars listed are for 2014.

Recession. The idea of a "progressive" system means that the state allocates a greater proportion of spending to districts serving students with fewer economic means and a "regressive" system keeps funds within systems, so a greater proportion of spending ends up in districts with more economic means. "Equitable" in this economic language means that the spending is 1:1 in that the same funds are flatly allocated per student no matter the economic status. Arizona became less progressive in its allocations since the Great Recession. Florida held steady at a 1:1 ratio. Michigan rescinded its regressive policies in aims for more flat allocation funding. North Carolina local politics held strong to regressive allocations, and thus the state and federal allocations countered this approach with modest progressive allocations. A report by the American Federation of Teachers (2018) accentuates the economic burdens of these years of stalled educational funding. Time will tell how COIVD-19 impacts educational funding.

Together, these four states provide rich contexts to demonstrate the national patterns that this study will test in the upcoming statistical analyses.

Coming Up Next

The next chapter frames the puzzle. It describes America's high school students in this early part of the 21st century: who they are, the variety of schools they attend, the courses they take, the students they see at school, and the range of academic abilities among the students. It is in this chapter that the students in the four spotlight states are described in more detail.

CHAPTER 3

The Landscape of College-Preparatory Curriculum in American High Schools

This chapter describes the backstory to the pipeline puzzle. In order to interpret the analyses in the upcoming chapters, we need to visualize the context of the types of districts and charter schools where American high school students study, the peers with whom they attend school, and the courses they take. These details will serve as a lens to interpret the patterns of racial, ethnic, and residential clusters to be used in the subsequent chapters.

AMERICAN HIGH SCHOOL LANDSCAPE

The American landscape is dotted with thousands of high schools, primarily divided into rural, town, suburban, and urban districts. Rural locales average one district high school and one charter school. Towns average 1–2 district high schools and one charter school. Suburban locales average 2–3 district high schools and one charter school. One-third of urban districts only have 1–2 high schools, and another half have between 3 and 11 high schools. Most urban districts only have one charter school (88%). By the numbers, the vast majority (70%) of U.S. districts operate only a single high school. Figure 3.1 darkens the landscape to map the expanse of single–high school districts across the U.S. landscape.

The American high school landscape is dominated by a monolithic secondary school structure, as seen in Figure 3.1. Of course, space on a map does not equate to student size. In 2013–14, the single–high school districts serve just over one-quarter of the high school students served in public traditional or charter schools.

As discussed in the prior chapters, American schooling in the 21st century emerges from decades of segregated schooling history, preceded by a century of schooling reserved only for the elite class of White peoples who owned land from Western European ancestry. The landscape of who attends which high schools and with which classmates reflects the U.S. history of residential

Figure 3.1. Distribution of U.S. Districts with One Single High School

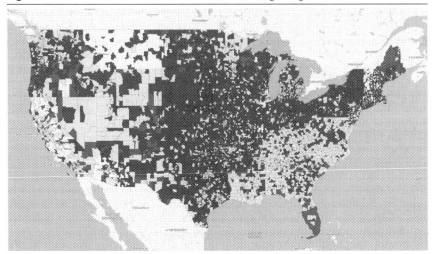

Note: Maps only illustrate unified school districts. Secondary-only districts are excluded from the illustration.

A larger and more detailed version of this map is available in the online Appendix, available at https://www.tcpress.com/the-fractured-college-prep-pipeline-9780807765029

segregation. As then expected, the average compositions of multi- and single-high school districts as well as charter schools vary widely, and the standard deviation numbers reflect this variation. For those interested in the differences among states, Table 3.1 provides these details.

Single–high school (single-HS) districts average 9–102[1] secondary-certified teachers among the 101–1,158 students in these single schools, as Table 3.1 shows. Over two-thirds of these single-HS districts have a school-wide Title I funding status. Half of these single-HS are comprised of hyper-homogeneous student populations where more than 90% of the students identify with the same, single racial or ethnic heritage, with four-tenths of these districts populated with more than 95% of students identifying with the one singular racial or ethnic heritage.

Ninety percent may seem like a high threshold to use. However, three-quarters of American students attend schools with racial concentrations of 75% or higher (EdBuild, 2019). This loosely translates to most schools as racially concentrated unless located in major metropolitan city districts. As such, the 90% threshold is adopted so as to isolate extreme cases of racial isolation. Orfield and Lee (2007) deem these "intensely segregated" schools.

Table 3.1. Average Organizational Composition of U.S. High Schools

	Multi–high school districts			Single–high school districts			Charter schools		
	median	*mean*	*s.d.*	*median*	*mean*	*s.d.*	*median*	*mean*	*s.d.*
High school students enrolled	1566	3463.55	9090.10	369	521.59	494.17	360	684.83	1689.74
Number of HS	3	4.59	11.79	1	1	0	1	1.33	1.70
Average HS enrollment	769.83	894.14	628.72	369.00	521.59	494.17	338.50	527.97	960.02
Number of secondary certified teachers	107.92	236.66	478.93	32.21	46.35	45.12	13.15	23.92	99.06
Full district Title I status		43.64%			68.22%			80.17%	
Rural		30.51%			59.93%			12.15%	
Town		23.57%			19.24%			8.22%	
Suburban		29.80%			19.18%			25.70%	
Urban		16.13%			1.65%			53.93%	
Student body demographics									
Hyper-homogeneous student body		22.40%			49.18%			20.67%	
American Indian/Alaska Native %	0.44%	2.51%	9.87%	0.32%	2.92%	10.71%	0.39%	2.07%	8.57%
Asian %	1.18%	3.05%	5.89%	0.71%	1.45%	3.14%	0.95%	2.72%	6.40%
Hispanic %	7.89%	17.96%	22.65%	3.14%	9.15%	15.71%	10.07%	22.31%	26.50%
Black, non-Hispanic %	3.60%	12.69%	19.75%	1.39%	5.90%	14.06%	10.04%	26.61%	32.42%
White, non-Hispanic %	67.50%	61.07%	28.38%	88.54%	78.50%	23.16%	45.19%	42.98%	33.87%
Native Hawaiian or Pacific Islander %	0.10%	0.28%	0.89%	0.00%	0.16%	0.47%	0.00%	0.31%	0.98%
Multiracial Amer %	1.72%	2.43%	2.71%	1.19%	1.92%	2.94%	1.99%	3.00%	4.12%
Limited English Proficiency %	1.64%	4.11%	7.11%	0.46%	2.07%	6.64%	0.71%	5.60%	13.24%
Special Education %	10.43%	10.99%	4.95%	12.02%	12.41%	6.27%	10.84%	12.29%	9.74%

Source: CRDC 2013–14 data.

Multi–high school (multi-HS) districts average 23–514 secondary-certified teachers among the 335–7,404 students distributed among the schools in the district (see Table 3.1). Over 40% of these multi-HS districts have Title I funding status throughout all the district schools. Only 31% of multi-HS districts have no Title I high schools districtwide. Fewer than one-quarter of these multi-HS are comprised of hyper-homogeneous student populations who identify with the same racial or ethnic heritage, with that same pattern of four-tenths of these districts enrolling more than 95% of students identifying with the one singular racial or ethnic heritage.

Moving on to charter schools, Table 3.1 shows these high schools average 0–43 secondary-certified teachers among the 91–1,284 students enrolled. Three-quarters of these charter high schools claim a Title I funding status. More than 20% of these charter schools are comprised of hyper-homogeneous student populations who identify with the same racial or ethnic heritage, with half of these districts enrolling more than 95% of students identifying with one singular racial or ethnic heritage.

About 9% of multi-HS districts include at least one charter school in their organizational design. These charter schools are contracted as a part of the district budget and use district resources to meet the needs of their students, such as sharing special education teacher hours. Thus, these charter schools are counted with traditional districts rather than as isolated educational entities operating under their own charter.

How common is it to see certain characteristics occur at the same time in a district or charter school? The overlap of organizational characteristics (expressed as correlation coefficients) shows that as the sheer number of high school students increases, so too does the number of high schools (see online Appendix Table A3.2). This seems like an obvious relationship that we would expect to make physical room for more students. The correlation also shows, perhaps less intuitively, that the number of students inside each of those school buildings also increases as district enrollment rises. Thus, even though more buildings house high school students in larger districts, the buildings in large districts enroll more students than smaller district high school buildings. This "big inside" school is more common in suburban high schools than any other locale.

The number of secondary teachers on the district roster rises with higher enrollments, and it is approximately proportional to the students-to-school relationship. Thus, more teachers in bigger districts and, like the students, more teachers per school building as the number of students in the building rises. While these may seem a bit obvious to describe, it helps in visualizing what schools look like inside differently sized districts.

Which students attend which districts? As Table 3.1 showed, single-HS districts serve higher rates of White, non-Hispanic students and occur most frequently in rural, town, and to some extent, suburban areas. There is a relationship between district composition and locale: Higher proportions of White, non-Hispanic students are more commonly found in rural districts, as corroborated by the correlation coefficients. In addition, hyper-homogeneous districts commonly associate with White, non-Hispanic student bodies. These hyper-homogeneous districts are found more often in rural areas than other areas. White, non-Hispanic student representation falls at a quick pace in urban districts.

In the suburbs, representation of Asian students rises at a faster pace. The proportion of Asian students in a district rises with school enrollment size.

Representations of Black, non-Hispanic students and, to a lesser extent, Hispanic students rise at a faster pace in urban areas than other areas. Hispanic student representation links to the population of limited English proficiency (LEP) students in the district. The proportion of White, non-Hispanic students falls when the LEP rate rises, but the White, non-Hispanic student population declines even more quickly as the proportion of Black, non-Hispanic and Hispanic students rise in the school than the rate of LEP.

Poverty is experienced by students in all school settings: rural to urban, White to Black, big to small. Despite popular assumptions, there is no district composition among the measures discussed in this book that relates noticeably more or less strongly to poverty than any other measure. The map in Figure 3.2 highlights the prevalence of students experiencing poverty across the United States. Districts (black areas) scatter across the United States where all schools receive Title I funds. Districts where no schools receive Title I funds (white areas) also scatter. Gray areas show districts where some, but not all the schools in the multi-HS districts receive Title I supplemental funding.

The distribution of poverty in the American high school landscape helps us understand the material and human resources available to schools. From the prior chapter, we know that research clearly shows that material resources, including successful or failing referenda, link to community wealth. Research also shows that teachers (as human resources) are less experienced and less certified in poorer districts (Carver-Thomas & Darling-Hammond, 2017; Gagnon & Mattingly, 2012; Ingersoll et al., 2014). Moreover, impoverished rural districts find extreme difficulty hiring teachers and often experience teacher shortages in classrooms (Malkus et al., 2015). Impoverished districts— from rural to urban—also experience higher rates of teacher attrition, which entails monetary replacement costs to districts (Barnes et al., 2007; Borman & Dowling, 2008) and interrupted learning costs to their students (Borman & Dowling, 2008; Henry & Redding, 2020; Ingersoll et al., 2014).

Figure 3.3 shows the distribution of the corresponding 8th-grade test scores (standardized to the National Assessment of Educational Progress scale) of two cohorts of students: those who would be 11th- and 12th-graders

Figure 3.2. District Concentration of High School Students Experiencing Poverty

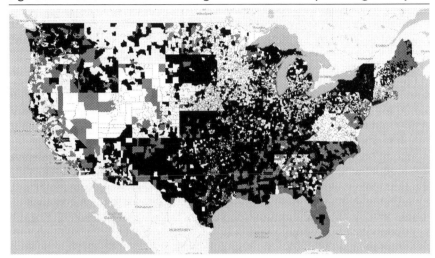

Notes: Maps only illustrate unified school districts. Secondary-only districts are excluded from the illustration. Some states, like West Virginia and Virginia, rarely allocate Title I funds to high schools.

A larger and more detailed version of this map is available in the online appendix, available at https://www.tcpress.com/the-fractured-college-prep-pipeline-9780807765029

during this 2013–14 year of CRDC data. These data pool the math and English/language arts scores of the districts among these two cohorts. The logic in this pooling of two cohorts is that juniors and seniors in high school are generally eligible for AP or IB courses and programming. Moreover, pooling two cohorts smooths out any anomalies of outlier cohorts.[2]

If all was equal in the American education system, we would expect that each state would have a mean of 0 and the same "spread" of scores throughout their state. The graph illustrates the unequal achievement levels of students throughout the United States. That is, students residing in Maryland are more likely to be going to school in a high-scoring district than students in South Dakota. Scholars Fahle and Reardon (2017) find that variation between districts gets 30% wider in the upper grades, so these 8th-grade data are the maximum width of variation for this dataset. Moreover, they find that variation between district scores strongly ties to White-Black and economic segregation.

Since this 2013–14 dataset, little in the American high school landscape has changed. Material and human resources remain stagnant (Snyder et al., 2019a). District configurations remain overwhelming stable (Snyder et al., 2019b, Table 214.10). The sheer number of charter high schools remains constant (Snyder et al., 2019b, Table 216.20); the new charter schools on the landscape generally replace ones that closed their doors (Snyder et al., 2019b, Table 216.95). The proportion of students of color in high school

Figure 3.3. Variation in Average 8th-Grade Achievement Scores in Districts, by State

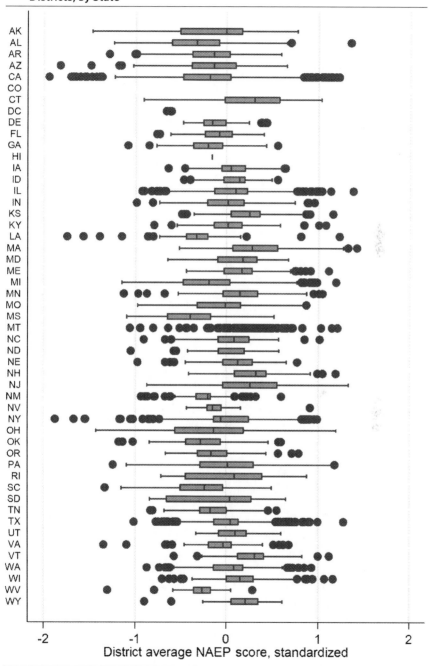

Source: Stanford Education Data Archives 8th-grade NAEP scores, 2010 & 2011.

grades has edged up five percentage points, but the proportions in districts remain relatively unchanged (Snyder et al., 2019b, Table 203.60). The proportions of limited English proficiency and special education have each edged up about half of a percentage point in the most recent 2018 data (Snyder et al., 2019b, Table 204.30). Overall, the 2013–14 student body well represents high school students at the time of this publication.

Since 2013–14, 3.8% of families continue to home school their high school–aged children (Snyder et al., 2019b, Table 206.10). This study cannot count these students in the analysis because there is no requirement to report to federal agencies about the curriculum taught in home schooling environments (USDOE, 2020a). Private high school enrollments remained stable in the past decade at 10% of the high school population (NCES, 2018). These students are also excluded from the analysis in this book.

SPOTLIGHT STATES: HIGH SCHOOL LANDSCAPE

Before moving on to describe AP and IB courses, let's paint the picture of what high school looks like in our four spotlight states. The online Appendix Tables A3.1–A3.4 show the numbers for these and all 50 states that support the pictures described in the following paragraphs.

Arizona's high schools mostly follow a single-HS district design. As the map showed in Figure 3.2, poverty is nearly everywhere across Arizonan districts and charter schools. Over one-third of districts are rural, and another one-third are in towns, while the other one-third is split evenly between suburban and urban areas. One in eight districts are hyper-homogeneous, but charter schools are less so. If we were to think of a high school senior class of 200 students, the student body would average 33 students with American Indian, 3 students with Asian, 66 students with Hispanic, 5 students with Black, non-Hispanic, 90 White, non-Hispanic, and 3 students with two or more racial heritages. The charter high schools enroll two-thirds fewer American Indian students in lieu of more Asian and Hispanic students, since there are few charter schools located in rural or town areas. Arizona's charter schools do not require teachers to have secondary certification, creating a major human resource difference in who is teaching the students in charter high school classrooms compared to traditional public classrooms.

Floridian high school students attend large districts with multiple high schools. Poverty varies within Floridian districts, in part due to the large size of districts, averaging 15 high schools, with a mix of some receiving Title I funds and others not. More than 40% of Florida's districts and charter schools are suburban, 30% rural, 20% township, and less than 10% urban. Due to the wide district boundaries, there is no hyper-homogeneity among the districts. Charter high schools only exist within districts. If we imagine a high school senior class of 200 students, the student body would average

1 student with American Indian, 3 students with Asian, 33 students with Hispanic, 37 students with Black, non-Hispanic, 120 students with White, non-Hispanic, and 6 students with two or more racial heritages.

Michigander high school students attend small districts, with an average of 1–2 high schools. Due to the small-sized districts separating communities, just over half of districts receive Title I funds in all of their district high schools. Nearly 90% of charter schools receive Title I funding. Nearly half of Michigan's districts are rural, 30% suburban, less than 18% township, and less than 7% urban. More than half of the charter schools are in urban areas, and 20% are located in rural areas. If we think of a high school senior class of 200 students, the student body would average 4 students with American Indian, 4 students with Asian, 10 students with Hispanic, 17 students with Black, non-Hispanic, 161 students with White, non-Hispanic, and 4 students with two or more racial heritages. Fully 86% of the Michigander students in charter high schools identify racially as White or Black (44% and 42%, respectively).

Michigan is the most hyper-homogeneous of the four spotlight states, with one in three districts and charters with hyper-segregated student bodies, as is common in historically segregated districts in the upper Midwest (Orfield, 1996). Let's take one county in Michigan to understand the racial differences of adjacent school districts. Kent County is a county mixed with urban, suburban, town, and rural districts. Nearly half of the districts in the county are hyper-homogeneous, with 11 districts enrolling 90% or more White, non-Hispanic high school students. This means that the "average class of 200" example above does not really materialize in almost any school in Michigan. Instead, half of the districts in Kent County would enroll at least 180 White, non-Hispanic students per class, and then the other districts would enroll fewer than 140 White, non-Hispanic students.

North Carolinian high school students attend medium-sized districts, averaging five high schools. More than two-thirds of districts receive Title I funds in all of their district high schools, as the map shows. Fewer than half of the charter schools receive Title I funding. Two in three North Carolinian districts and 2 in 5 charter schools are rural, with the rest about equally distributed among the other three locales. Like Florida and other countywide Southern districts, it is rare to encounter a hyper-homogeneous district or charter school in North Carolina. If we imagine our class of 200 high school seniors, the student body would average 4 students with American Indian, 3 students with Asian, 20 students with Hispanic, 51 students with Black, non-Hispanic, 116 students with White, non-Hispanic, and 6 students with two or more racial heritages. Charter school student bodies enroll 10 percentage points more White, non-Hispanic and half as many Hispanic students.

Among these four spotlight states, the representation of Native Hawaiian and Other Pacific Islander students is minuscule. In Hawaii and the Western states of Alaska, California, Idaho, Nevada, Oregon, Utah, and Washington, these students are represented more.

In each of these four spotlight states, there is about 10–11% special education students and 2% with limited English proficiency (LEP) needs. However, this low percentage of LEP in Arizona is not accurate because the state was cited in 2016 by the Department of Justice for years of artificially deeming English-language learners proficient (USDOJ Civil Rights Division, 2016).

Looking at the four spotlight states, we see that the relationships of size to number of school buildings and number of secondary teachers act like the national correlations. Appendix Tables A3.3–A3.6 (online) show the correlation matrices for each spotlight state.

The correlations in Arizona work very similarly to the national ones. The two differences are: In Arizona, instead of a reduction of White, non-Hispanic student representation falling with the rise of Black, non-Hispanic students, it instead falls with the rise of American Indian student representation. Arizona also shows little correlation of Hispanic student representation link to LEP rates, but this is due to the failure to accurately classify LEP needs of students, as discussed in the above paragraph.

Florida's district configurations are closely tied to size differences. Bigger districts tend to be more suburban and enroll greater proportions of Asian, Hispanic, and LEP students as well as fewer White, non-Hispanic students. In Florida and North Carolina, the LEP rate is very closely tied to the Hispanic student enrollment rates.

Michigan's and North Carolina's correlations are nearly identical to the national ones, with the exception of a major racial Black-White difference. In both states, the rate of White, non-Hispanic student populations is a –0.90 match to the rate of Black, non-Hispanic students. This statistic (correlation coefficient) is interpreted to mean that for every percentage-point increase in Black, non-Hispanic high school students in the district, there is nearly a mirror image drop in the percentage of White, non-Hispanic high school students represented in the same district. For Michigan, part of this relationship is tied to a rural/urban divide, but that is not the case in North Carolina. To illustrate this correlation, Figure 3.3 plots the districts' high school population compositions for Michigan and North Carolina in this dataset.

To illustrate the correlation, let's look at four districts around the Chapel Hill area of North Carolina: the city district plus the three county districts in which the city resides. Three of the districts average majority (54–67%) White, non-Hispanic high school students, while Durham Public Schools averages 20% White, non-Hispanic. Durham Public Schools enrolls the mirror image of 54% Black, non-Hispanic high school students, demonstrating that correlation shown in Figure 3.4. Each of these four districts enroll 12–23% Hispanic high school students.

Durham Public Schools enrolls three times more students than either of the other three districts. Inside the district, the representation stays quite even across all schools. Together, it enrolls 54% Black, non-Hispanic students and 20% each Hispanic and White, non-Hispanic students. While

Figure 3.4. Correlation of High School Student Representation in Michigan and North Carolina Districts

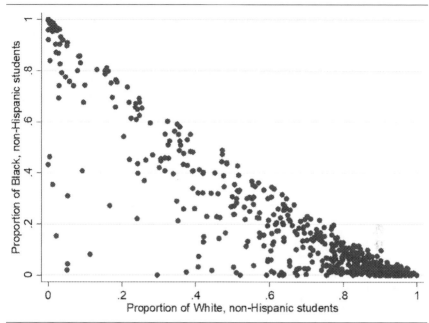

Source: CRDC 2013–14 data.

three of its high schools enroll 75–85% Black, non-Hispanic students, none enroll more than one-third White, non-Hispanic students. Only two schools enroll notably lower proportions of Hispanic students. Overall, the transfer request policies used by Durham Public Schools (Durham Public Schools, 2020; website: https://www.dpsnc.net/site/Default.aspx?PageID=210) appear to reduce intra-district segregation.

Comparatively, the biggest and most diverse district in Kent County, Grand Rapids Public Schools, enrolls 24% White, non-Hispanic, 40% Black, non-Hispanic, and 27% Hispanic high school students among its six high schools. On the surface, it looks quite diverse. However, when looking at the enrollment of its six high schools, two schools enroll 70% Black, non-Hispanic students, one enrolls 55% White, non-Hispanic students, one enrolls 45% Hispanic students, and one enrolls 80% Hispanic and Black, non-Hispanic students. Only the one Montessori high school enrollment roughly reflects the total high school population in the district. This within-district segregation is commonplace in districts that offer annual intradistrict open enrollment with sibling preferences (Lee & Lubienski, 2011; Posey-Maddox, 2014), as Grand Rapids Public Schools does (Grand Rapids Public Schools, 2020).

Comparisons in districts like these in Michigan and North Carolina show us where the impact of *Brown v. Board of Education* and the *Milliken v.*

Bradley court rulings can be differently experienced by way of the interdistrict versus intradistrict segregation in the United States. Moreover, the expanse of the district in a land area also plays a role because the catchment zone of larger-spatial districts like Chatham and Orange County Schools in North Carolina induces integration across residential segregation much more so than the small districts in Michigan that retain racialized residential boundaries.

Lastly, Arizona and Michigan districts average lower (–0.15 and –0.20 s.d., respectively) than the national average on achievement. Florida scores slightly below average (–0.09 s.d.). North Carolina districts score slightly above average (0.06 s.d.) compared to the U.S. average. The range of district scores is widest for Michigan, Arizona is moderately wide, and the range of scores in the southern states of Florida and North Carolina are relatively narrow.

COLLEGE-PREP CURRICULUM LANDSCAPE

Now that we have a picture of the districts, high schools, and classrooms, the discussion turns to describing the college-prep curriculum. How does a "college-prep class" work? What makes it different than other honors courses in high school? How has college prep changed in this 21st century?

Discussions on college-prep coursework typically include three types of courses: Advanced Placement (AP), International Baccalaureate (IB), and "dual enrollment." As explained in the prior chapter, this study excludes dual enrollment from the discussion here because this Civil Rights Data Collection (CRDC) database is unable to distinguish college-prep from career-prep courses included in the dual enrollment definition. To avoid inducing error, it is excluded from this discussion.

The following paragraphs review the content coverage and rigor of AP and IB courses and explain how these courses match the "college for all" rhetoric. In doing so, we can understand what the rhetoric looks and feels like in high school classes today.

The College Board (the management organization of AP) explains that the distinguishing features of Advanced Placement courses are that the content specifically aligned to a corresponding college-level introductory discipline-specific course (College Board, 2020, https://apcentral.collegeboard.org/about-ap/ap-a-glance). The International Baccalaureate organization explains that it is the service and research aspects of the learning that distinguishes their courses (Pannoni & Moody, 2019). Notably different between AP and IB is the interdisciplinary learning of IB compared to the college-curriculum knowledge acquisition of AP. The IB Diploma Programme—the one most popular in high school—is reserved for 16–19-year-old students, whereas any student of any age can enroll in an AP course if they meet the prerequisites of their individual schools. In addition, there is no prescribed curriculum for AP courses, but rather they aim to achieve shared learning outcomes (College Board, 2020, https://apcentral.collegeboard.org/about-ap/ap-a-glance). In IB, the teachers follow a prescriptive curriculum (International Baccalaureate Organization, 2020, https://www.ibo.org/professional-development/professional-certificates /ib-educator-certificates/). The stress on language and history in IB separates it from AP, but the math and science offerings are quite comparable (Hanover Research, 2010). Together, AP and IB stand out from "honors" courses because the course content covered is supposed to be standardized across courses across schools. For each, external exams assess mastery of learning in an absolute comparative context rather than the internally relative standards used for honors courses in schools.

There is also a push to democratize access to college-prep courses. As Donaldson (2017) explains,

> State and national-level policies like the No Child Left Behind Act, Every Student Succeeds Act, and My Brother's Keeper Initiative have encouraged the democratization of advanced courses in order to equalize and provide opportunities for a broader range of students, namely those from historically underrepresented groups. For example, Part G of NCLB, the Access to High Standards Act, called for increasing the number of students who have access to advanced placement programs, increasing preparation for these programs as early as middle school, providing access at schools that do not have these types of courses, increasing the number of students taking advanced course exams in the aims of earning college credit, and subsidizing testing fees for low-income students (No Child Left Behind Act 2002, 20 U.S.C. 6532). (p. 49)

To show their commitment to the democratization of college-prep learning opportunities, Donaldson (2017) further evidences that

> The College Board routinely publishes reports on [the] "equity gap" that exists among racial/ethnic groups in who takes AP coursework and exams as well as exam results (e.g. The College Board 2012, 2014b). For example, the College Board (2014b) estimates only four out of 10 Latinx students and three out of 10 Black students who have the [academic] potential to take AP math coursework do so. In addition, Black students were the most underrepresented group among AP exam takers (The College Board 2014b). Given these gaps, combined with the beneficial outcomes of advanced course taking, policies have explicitly called to increase access to these courses. (p. 49)

The Elementary and Secondary Education Act (ESEA) laws and "college for all"–related policies rapidly increased AP participation since the turn of the century (Geiser & Santelices, 2006; Wildhagen, 2014), along with the acceleration of adopting IB programming (Donaldson, 2017). Just looking at AP exam data shows nearly a doubling of AP in the decade since 2003 (see Figure 3.5).

Figure 3.5. Number of High School Graduates Taking AP Exam

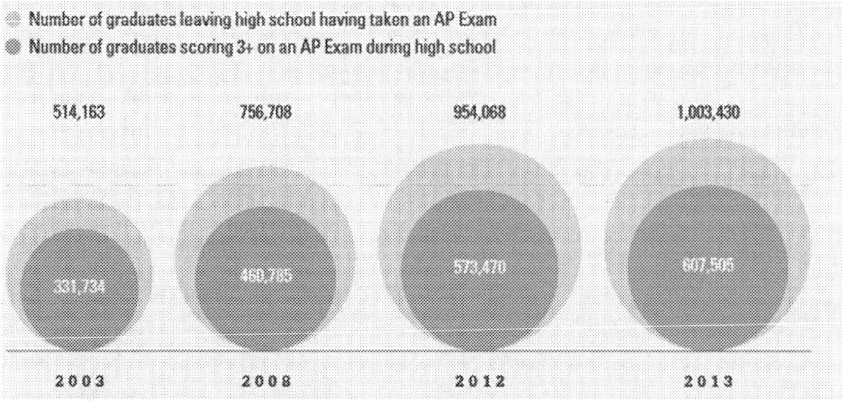

- Number of graduates leaving high school having taken an AP Exam
- Number of graduates scoring 3+ on an AP Exam during high school

514,163	756,708	954,068	1,003,430
331,734	460,785	573,470	607,505
2003	2008	2012	2013

Source: College Board (2014, p. 10).

In addition to the increasing numbers of districts offering these college-prep courses, Figure 3.6 shows a near doubling in the variety of AP courses available to students within a school (Geiser & Santelices, 2006; Judson & Hobson, 2015). However, Wildhagen (2014) shows that democratization also leads to decreasing exchange value in the college marketplace.

> The College Board only tracks numbers by student counts of exam takers. These graphics therefore underrepresent students in the classroom seats because not all students take the AP exams, as subsequent chapters will evidence.

Counts on U.S. students enrolled in IB are difficult to pin down, as the IB organization keeps its enrollment information away from public reporting. From the CRDC data, we know that the students enrolled in IB courses (which are not necessarily part of the IB Diploma Programme) numbered more than 185,000 students in 2013–14 and dropped slightly to over 153,000 in 2015–16. Figure 3.7 shows, however, the rapid rise of IB in schools across the United States in the 21st century. In the United States, there has been "more than a 200 percent increase in the number of [International Baccalaureate Diploma Programme schools] from 2000 to 2016, from nearly 300 to 900 schools" (Donaldson, 2017, p.116).

As the above paragraphs and figures show, the prevalence of AP is much greater than IB. In fact, there are only 101 public high schools (one-third of which are charter schools) in this 2013–14 dataset that only deliver IB curriculum. When IB is delivered, 88% of schools that deliver IB also offer AP courses in the school's course bulletin.

Figure 3.6. Numbers of High School Graduates Taking AP Exam, by Subject Area

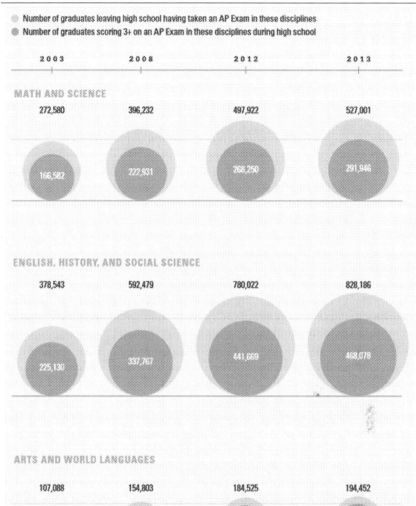

○ Number of graduates leaving high school having taken an AP Exam in these disciplines
● Number of graduates scoring 3+ on an AP Exam in these disciplines during high school

2003	2008	2012	2013

MATH AND SCIENCE

| 272,580 | 396,232 | 497,922 | 527,001 |
| 166,582 | 222,931 | 268,250 | 291,946 |

ENGLISH, HISTORY, AND SOCIAL SCIENCE

| 378,543 | 592,479 | 780,022 | 828,186 |
| 225,130 | 337,767 | 441,669 | 468,078 |

ARTS AND WORLD LANGUAGES

| 107,088 | 154,803 | 184,525 | 194,452 |
| 76,484 | 102,044 | 129,238 | 139,488 |

Source: College Board (2014, p. 14).

Figure 3.7. Number of U.S. High Schools Offering International Baccalaureate Degree Programs

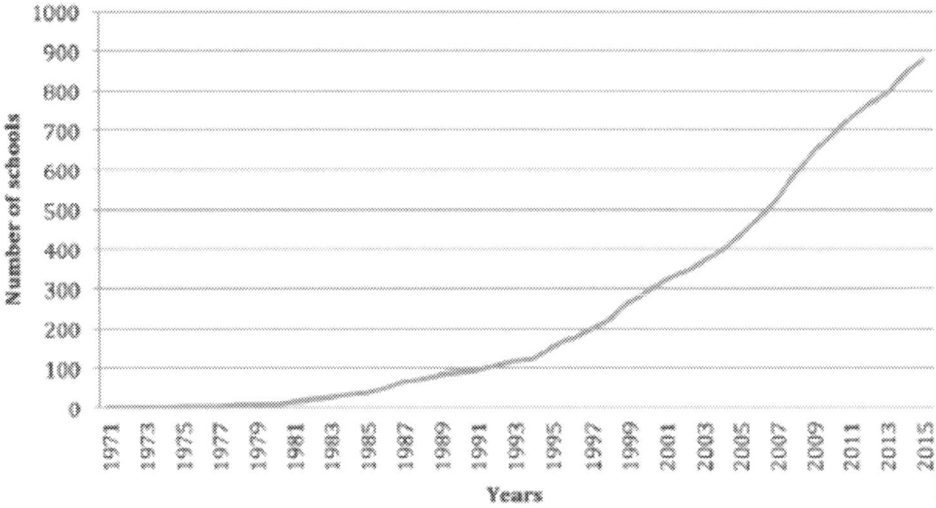

Source: Donaldson (2017, p. 117).

A note about calculus: It could be the case that middle school courses affect the sequencing needed to take college-prep courses in high school. While this could be a factor for AP Calculus, it is not the case that English, history, science, psychology, and other AP or IB courses need specific prerequisites from middle school years to ready students for high school college-prep schedules. Even with calculus, high school students could, in theory, double up Algebra I or II with geometry to get to calculus in high school even if they did not get algebra in their 8th-grade year. In fact, there appears to be no relationship between 8th-grade placement and AP placement (Loveless, 2016).

Nonetheless, to address this matter head-on with empirical evidence instead of a theoretical rationale, the analyses find that only 3% of districts in the whole 2013–14 dataset *solely* offer calculus as the only college-prep course. Since this number is so low and the models combine all AP and IB courses to test general trends in the college-prep pipeline, the caveat of the middle school course sequencing does not impact the statistical results.

Theoretically, the caveat of calculus actually bolsters the argument since Domina and colleagues (2016) show strong evidence of counterfeit 8th-grade algebra coursework in California, where the state mandated all 8th-grade students learn algebra. Since this mandate, the coverage of algebraic material in 8th grade has become widely varied and shown no significant impact on math scores nor high school math achievement (Domina et al., 2016).

THE COLLEGE-PREPARATORY PIPELINE

How do students get into college-prep (CP) classes? First, districts need to offer CP courses; then students need to register to take them. These courses exist alongside other courses needed for graduation in the Academic Bulletin. Often, to register for these classes, schools require certain prerequisite courses, minimum grade point averages, and/or teacher signatures (Kelly, 2007; Kelly & Price, 2011). Since many require prerequisites, students often do not participate in CP until their 11th- and 12th-grade years.

Interlocked stages create the college-prep curricular pipeline. These three stages structure the 21st-century CP opportunities to learn in American high schools. Figure 3.8 shows these stages:

Stage 1, Access: Whether or not students are enrolled in districts that have AP or IB offerings.
Stage 2, Participation: Which students in the district participate in these courses.
Stage 3, Quality: How well students demonstrate mastery of the learned material.

Remaining in the pipeline at each stage, versus an exit from it, compounds educational inequality and contributes to disparities in college preparation. Each pipeline stage leaks out some students from inside the pipeline who do not advance to the next stage. In addition, Stages 2 and 3 structurally flush certain students entirely out of the pipeline using exclusionary organizational designs. The subsequent chapters will describe the factors that create flushes versus leaks and how students are differentially impacted by leaks and flushes, as these are important parts of this pipeline puzzle.

Figure 3.8. College-Preparatory Curricular Pipeline

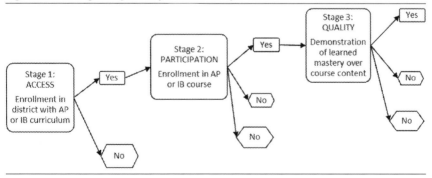

Figure 3.9. Flow of the College-Prep Curricular Pipeline in the United States

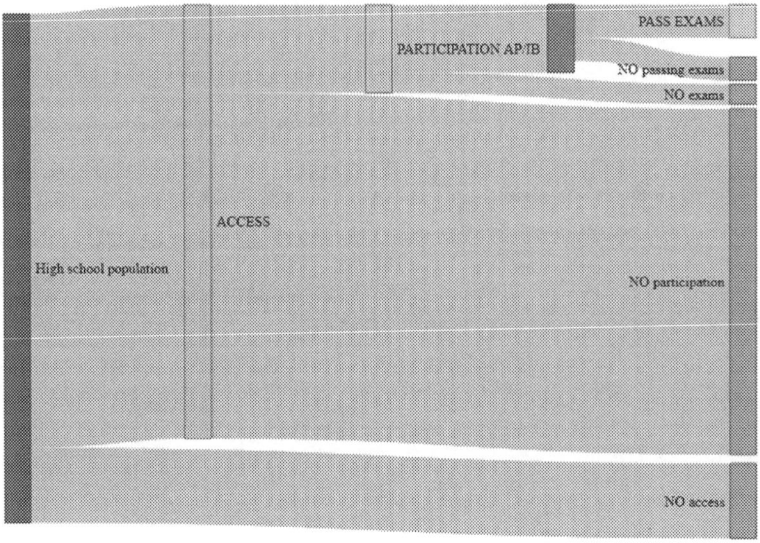

Source: CRDC 2013–14 data.

Stage 1, 1 in 9 American high school students leak out because they attend district or charter schools with neither college-prep option, as illustrated in Figure 3.9. Among these students with access, only a select 1 in 6 participate in at least one college-prep course at Stage 2. In particular, only 1 in 100 are enrolled in any IB course. Stage 2 flushes out 1 in 19 students because their district school specifically offers no AP or IB courses. At Stage 3, nearly 1 in 4 students get flushed out because they sit in AP classrooms where no AP exam is proctored to test the quality of their learning. Among those who take an exam at Stage 3, about 6 in 10 earn a passing score. The other 4 in 10 leak out of the pipeline because they failed to pass any exam. By the end of the pipeline, only 1 in 13 students enrolled in regular high schools earned an IB or AP course credential accepted by (most) postsecondary institutions for credit toward a bachelor's degree graduation.

SPOTLIGHT STATES: THE AP AND IB LANDSCAPE

Even though AP and IB are not regulated by state standards or jurisdictions, the access, participation, and quality of these college-prep curricula vary by state. The biggest reason for this is funding. Some states, like Florida, partially fund AP and IB curriculum through the state budget (Education

Commission, 2020). Arizona follows no such model; it does not fund any AP or IB curriculum (Education Commission, 2020), leaving it solely up to its districts to coordinate.

Florida's budget provides professional development funding for teachers to become certified instructors in AP or IB (Education Commission, 2020). In the other three states, these development funds are not available via legislative budget allocations, leaving the choice to train teachers and the funding for that training up to local schools. Or teachers need their own money and know-how to develop the instructor skills necessary to teach these courses.

In all states, including these four spotlight states, the College Board does offer funding to subsidize costs associated with taking AP exams (Education Commission, 2020). States like Florida, Michigan, and North Carolina also add further funds to subsidize exam costs for qualified students from low-income households (Education Commission, 2020). This book will show how these subsidies matter for students and their opportunities to gain the college-prep credential. It is important to remember that these subsidies at Stage 3 do rest on the premise that students participate in these courses at Stage 2, and these courses are available to students in Stage 1.

COMING UP NEXT

The next chapter puts together the access portion of the puzzle as we look into Stage 1: whether or not students attend a district or charter school with AP or IB curriculum. This next chapter shows how material and human resource constraints partially explain why some districts and charter schools cannot offer AP or IB courses. It also shows which students leak out of the pipeline at this first stage simply because they reside in one district instead of another.

CHAPTER 4

The Foundation of Access to Opportunity

As the prior chapter framed, there are three stages along the college-prep pipeline that interlock in the puzzle to explain counterfeit credentials and opportunities to learn. In order for students to start the journey along the pipeline, they first need *access* to the prep courses. A student needs to be enrolled in a district that actually offers college-prep curriculum in order to even have a chance at taking these courses. This first stage of the pipeline, when districts do and do not offer college-prep coursework, is the focus of this chapter.

As discussed earlier, there has been a steady push for an increase in the college readiness curriculum available to high school students. Chapter 3 showed a steady rise in access to Advanced Placement (AP). The rise became steeper in the past 20 years (Geiser & Santelices, 2006; Judson & Hobson, 2015; Wildhagen, 2014). More recently, International Baccalaureate (IB) course offerings for high school students also began to accelerate in availability across the nation (Donaldson, 2017). The access to AP and IB courses increased in sheer number of districts offering these college-prep courses and in the variety of courses available to students within a school (Donaldson, 2017; Geiser & Santelices, 2006; Judson & Hobson, 2015).

Recall from Chapter 2, this pattern of offering AP and IB coincides with the rise of the "college for all" mentality nationwide (Goyette, 2008; Jacob et al., 2017; Klugman, 2012; Wildhagen, 2014). In effect, the rise in the accessibility and relative normativity of college-prep curriculum has increased the average of high school course-taking expectations in this century.

HISTORICAL BACKGROUND ON ACCESS TO CURRICULUM

To discuss this aspect of access, it is necessary to piece together some historical context. During the Jim Crow and residential redlining eras, per-pupil funding allowances were vastly different; and, as a result, the opportunities for curriculum choices were vastly different depending on the racial composition of a given school (Graham, 2005; Mickelson, 2001; Smith & Crosby, 2008; Tyack, 1974; Walters, 2000). The end to de jure segregated schooling in post-*Brown v. Board of Education* altered the manner in which access to curriculum occurred as de facto policy (Chermerinsky, 2002; Clotfelter, 2004; Orfield, 1996).

De facto access today describes how district context impacts students' access to differentiated curriculum (Klopfenstein, 2004; Siegel-Hawley et al., 2018). In schools serving marginalized students, there are often human resources issues where the teacher pool is made up of more novice and fewer advanced-degreed teachers. The end result is that these districts lack teachers who are trained to teach advanced college-prep courses (Gagnon & Mattingly, 2012; Lankford et al., 2002; U.S. Department of Education Office for Civil Rights, 2014).

In addition, rural districts often do not have enough numbers of students to offer differentiated sections of a course subject, such as an honors history and a regular history course (Cisneros et al., 2014; Gagnon & Mattingly, 2016; Iatarola et al., 2017; Lee et al., 2000; Loveless, 1999; Siegel-Hawley et al., 2018). Moreover, distances are too far to travel for individual students to attend courses at nearby colleges, and unreliable Internet connections in rural America make distance learning inaccessible (KewalRamani et al., 2018). These issues especially impact Native American students, who predominantly attend schools in rural areas (Apthorp, 2016; Christenson et al., 1996; DeVoe & Darling-Churchill, 2008; Pavel & Curtin, 1997).

In urban districts, the human resources pool is larger, but these extra resources are primarily used to attend to other student needs besides college-preparatory work. Human resources seldom remain to disperse to optional needs of advanced curriculum offerings (Iatarola et al., 2017).

Although the structural circumstances differ between the rural and urban districts, the access to college-prep curriculum is quite similar: It is often the organization's financial and human resource demands that constrain students' access to curricular educational opportunities (Cisneros et al., 2014; Gagnon & Mattingly, 2016; Iatarola et al., 2017; Klopfenstein, 2004; Siegel-Hawley et al., 2018).

DISTRICT ACCESS IN THE UNITED STATES

To help visualize the various offerings in college-preparatory work across the United States, let's look at a nationwide map illustrating basic availability of these courses in Figure 4.1. All unshaded areas represent districts with no options for AP or IB courses in 2013–14. While these courses might be listed in the Academic Bulletin of a given district, the district remains unshaded if no course was taught in the school year. Of the nearly 11,000 districts that serve high school students in the United States, over 30% report offering no AP or IB courses. The map allows us to see how these districts primarily cluster in the Plains states. Figure 4.2 lists the proportion of

Figure 4.1. Map of College Prep Offerings Across U.S. Districts

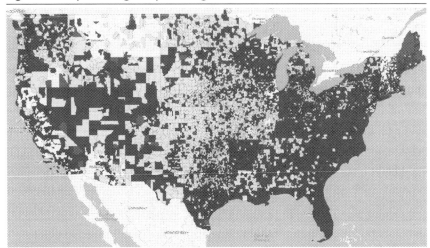

Alaska: Two-thirds of districts do not have access; Hawaii: one single district has access.

Note: Dark areas show where AP or IB is offered in at least one high school in the district; light areas denote no AP or IB offered in the district. Maps only illustrate unified school districts. Secondary-only districts are excluded from the illustration.

Source: Civil Rights Data Collection, 2013–14.

A larger and more detailed version of this map is available in the online appendix, available for free at https://www.tcpress.com/the-fractured-college-prep-pipeline -9780807765029

districts per state with no AP or IB curricula, which underscores the trends shown on the map.

Charter high schools are difficult to show on a map since there would be 1,558 individual dots across the map, so these schools are visualized using the proportion of charter schools per state that do not offer any AP or IB courses in their high schools. The simple majority of charter high schools in the United States (n=763) do not offer any AP or IB curricula. Figure 4.3 shows that more than half of the charter schools that *do not* offer college prep cluster in the Northeast and upper-midwestern states (Maine, New Hampshire, Rhode Island, Delaware, New York, New Jersey; Ohio, Minnesota, Iowa, Michigan, Indiana, Pennsylvania) as well as in the West (North Dakota, Utah, Missouri, Wyoming, Arizona, Texas, New Mexico). Interestingly, looking at Figures 4.2 and 4.3 together, the states where high numbers of charter schools do not offer AP or IB are not the same as the states where high numbers of districts do not offer AP or IB. As the upcoming analyses will show, the traditional districts' access is greatly affected by locale, but this is less the case with charter schools.

The 30% of the nation's districts and the half of charter schools that serve high school students that report no college-prep curriculum account

TEACHERS COLLEGE PRESS

TEACHERS COLLEGE | COLUMBIA UNIVERSITY

PRESS RELEASE

THE FRACTURED COLLEGE PREP PIPELINE

Hoarding Opportunities to Learn

Heather E. Price

March 2021 / 176 pp. / Paperback/ 9780807765029
List Price: $38.95

Description

This book walks readers through the stages of the high school college prep pipeline that introduce interlocked structural barriers to student achievement. The author shows how these barriers reinforce segregated structures that unfairly distribute the public good of education to some students and not others. Price argues that the college prep pipeline of Advanced Placement and International Baccalaureate coursework in American high schools constitutes a new form of tracking in the 21st century. Even further, this new tracking introduces a façade of "college readiness" that veils the unequal learning opportunities that send some students out into the college world with pockets full of counterfeit credentials that serve only to reinforce the historically oppressive system. Whether intentional or not, this new form of tracking is embedded in schools across the United States and has lifetime consequences for individual students that

Book Features

- Follows all the stages in the college prep pipeline, from access to curriculum to participation in classes to demonstration of mastery of the course content.
- Provides a more valid measure of quality by using the national tests of College Board Advanced Placement to compare the learning outcomes of students enrolled in the same classes across the nation.
- Uses Arizona, Florida, Michigan, and North Carolina as case studies that exemplify the variation in practice and policy across the United States.
- Compares public districts to charter high schools, showing how the rise in school choice policies hinders integration efforts.

THE
FRACTURED
COLLEGE
PREP
PIPELINE

HOARDING
OPPORTUNITIES
TO LEARN

HEATHER E. PRICE

Heather E. Price is assistant professor of leadership studies doctoral program with concurrent appointment in the Social, Behavioral, and Forensic Sciences department at Marian University.

For more information, please contact:

Emily Freyer

Teachers College Press

freyer@tc.edu

Figure 4.2. Proportion of Districts with No Access to AP or IB Courses

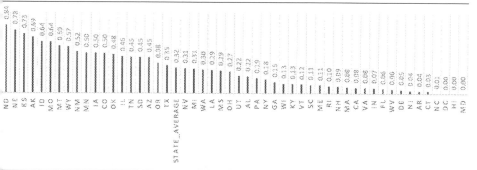

Note: Hawaii is one single district across all islands.
Source: Civil Rights Data Collection, 2013–14.

Figure 4.3. Proportion of Charter Schools with No Access to AP or IB Courses

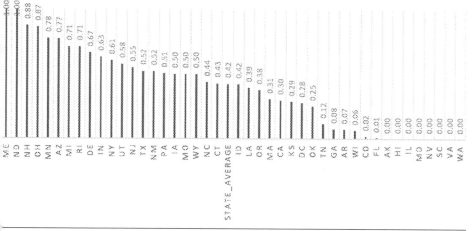

Note: The states of AL, KY, MS, MT, NE, ND, SD, VT, WA, and WV had no charter schools in ՏY 2013–14 (NCES, 2016).
Source: Civil Rights Data Collection, 2013–14.

for nearly 9,000 high schools across the nation. The vast majority of these districts without access have small infrastructures, averaging one to two high schools per district.

DISTRICT RESOURCES: CONCENTRATION vs. DILUTION

When we compare the districts without any available college-prep courses to those districts with college prep, some particular aspects of these districts'

Figure 4.4. Students' Access to AP or IB in Their District by Human Resources

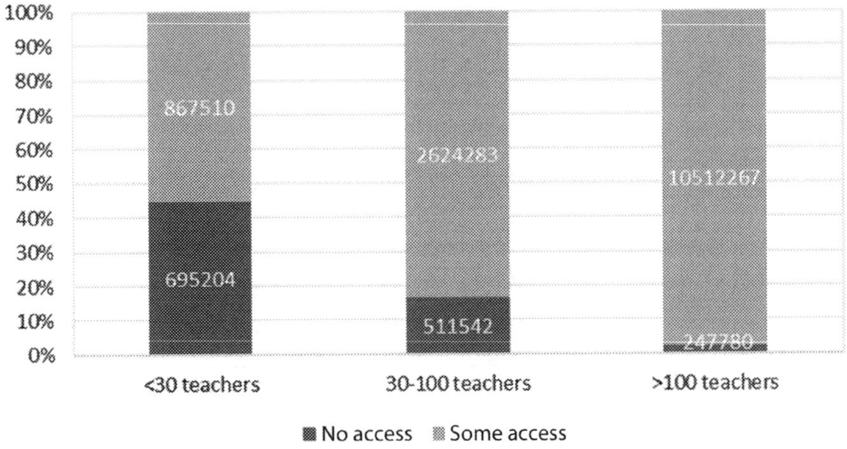

Source: Civil Rights Data Collection, 2013–14.

profiles stand out. As the following analyses will show, the districts without access are substantially more rural, more financially strained, and smaller.

To a great degree, the number of teachers that are licensed in a district to specifically teach high school grade levels determines the availability of human resources to teach college-preparatory coursework. We can see in Figure 4.4 that nearly half of the students who attend districts that have fewer than 30 teachers with a secondary high school teaching license do not have access to AP or IB in their high schools. Students attending districts with a moderate human resource base have substantially more access to AP or IB, and students in districts with a large pool of certified teachers experience nearly no lack of access to these courses.

> Note about teachers: The small number of secondary-certified teachers is not concentrated in districts that only have one high school. Half of all districts with only one high school employ more than 30 teachers with secondary certifications. However, it is the case, as discussed earlier in the chapter, that the human resources available for districts to draw on (i.e., teachers with proper qualifications to teach CP courses) are much more restricted in rural areas than in larger locales.
>
> Also, the 30- and 100-teacher cutpoints are pragmatically important to reduce multicollinearity. If a continuous count of teachers were used, it would coincide too much with student population size. The 30 and 100 empirically show "natural cutpoints" in the data. These are not intended to become target numbers for policies on teacher staffing.

Figure 4.5. Students' Access to AP or IB in Their District by Locale

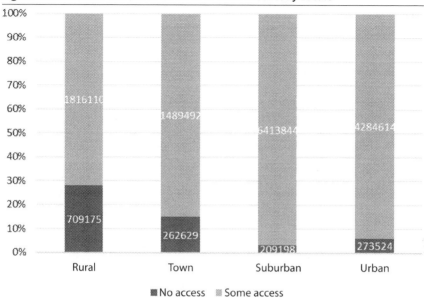

Source: Civil Rights Data Collection, 2013–14.

As seen in Figure 4.5, nearly 30% of students who attend public school districts in rural America had no AP or IB courses offered. Students in nearby towns have double the access as their rural counterparts. This starkly compares to the fact that 1 in 20 urban students lack access, while nearly no students who live in the suburbs lack access to AP or IB. Half of all charter schools (not shown here) are urban. The urban charter students have less access than the charter school students living elsewhere.

One might assume that locale is just a signal of the level of poverty in the district. As Figure 4.6 shows, slight disparity in access exists if a public district enrolls more than 40% impoverished students.[1] However, impact of student poverty on access to AP and IB is *four times greater* if a student attends a charter school that qualifies for Title I funding than if they attend a charter school with fewer low-income students.

The counterargument to this study's resource-based theory could postulate that districts may not have "demand" for AP or IB courses if their students are less academically ready to take these courses. That is, there would be no reason to supply AP or IB in districts whose students generally score lower on the achievement tests. Figure 4.7 shows how the ability argument looks between states.[2] Clearly, there are districts with relatively below-average-ability-scoring students that still provide AP or IB access, and there are districts with above-average-ability-scoring students that do not provide access. This means that students attending above-average districts in the

Figure 4.6. Students' Access to AP or IB in Their District by Material Resources

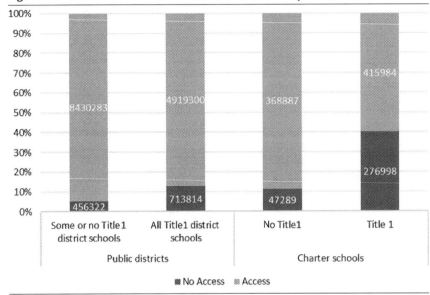

Source: Civil Rights Data Collection, 2013–14.

American Northeast, for example, may have no access to AP or IB, whereas if they attended below-average districts in the American South, they may indeed have access to these courses.

As noted in Chapter 2, AP and IB courses do not rely on state standards, so the state boundaries should not be a hindrance to access to these courses, yet the figures and the map clearly show that a student's access to AP and IB curricula depends on the state where they live. It then begs the question about how the allocation of resources among districts provide this curricular access to some students but not others.

Given the interrelatedness of the resources involved, logistic regression models identify the material and human resources that stand out as contributors to the identified disparities in access. When we look at all of these resources together, differences in poverty reveal as an artifact of locale (see online Table A4.1). It is locale that accounts for the disparity, not poverty (see online Tables A4.1, A4.2).

The human resource pool of teachers also matters whatever the poverty level. Access is significantly lower in districts and charter schools with only a handful of secondary-certified teachers (see online Tables A4.1, A4.2). For urban districts, the likelihood of access decreases by 33% once human resources are accounted.

Lastly, there is still much variation across districts within states, despite the average ability differences between states. The model thus averages

Figure 4.7. Average Achievement Score Differences Between Districts With or Without Access, by State

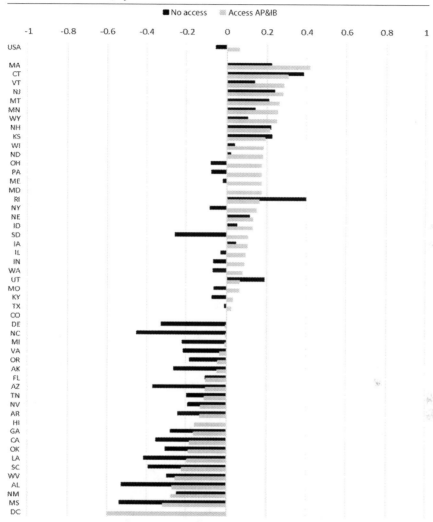

Note: SEDA 8th-grade NAEP data used from 2009–10 and 2010–11 to capture the achievement levels of the high school students in those districts during the 2013–14 college-prep school year. Colorado has no 8th-grade achievement SEDA data for these school years.

achievement score of districts' students, no matter the state,[3] to test whether or not there is an "ability demand" for districts to offer AP or IB courses.[4] Indeed, districts whose students score an average of a whole standard deviation higher than the national average on 8th-grade achievement tests are more likely to offer AP or IB than other districts (see model 6 in online Tables A4.1 and A4.2).

Importantly, this ability argument does not dilute the importance of resources. Student achievement may contribute to the demand for AP or IB, but scant human and material resources of districts preclude the adoption of these courses, independent of the students' academic abilities.[5] When all of these factors are looked at together (model 7 in online Tables A4.1 and A4.2), the impact of human and material resources strengthens, and the impact of ability and student composition of the districts weakens. The locale of a district in rural/town areas and the human resources available in the form of qualified teachers to teach the courses strongly explain the differences between those districts with or without any AP or IB. It does not prove case that lack of access relates to the students' socio-demographics per se, but rather access shows to be mostly a spatial proximity inequality issue.

UNEQUAL CONSEQUENCES FOR STUDENTS WITHOUT ACCESS

Although many districts or charter schools do not offer college-prep curriculum in their high schools, these locales enroll fewer high school students than locales with access. In fact, 90% of high school students are enrolled in districts or charter schools that offer some college-prep curriculum, while 10% attend schools that do not.

However, when we look at the students who attend districts with no college prep compared to the other 90% of American high school students, racialized disparities surface. Figure 4.8 shows that nearly 1 in 4 students of American Indian or Alaska Native ancestry lack access to college prep in their district. White, non-Hispanic students—the next-largest group without access—come in at half the rate, with a rate of 1 in 8.

Among the nearly 1.5 million students who attend districts with no access, 3% are American Indian or Alaskan Native. Nationally, these students comprise only 1.2% of the high school population (NCES, 2017, Table 203.60). This means that these students are 2.4 times more likely to lack access to college-prep coursework in their districts compared to other high school students. White, non-Hispanic students—the next-largest group without access—comprise 65% of the high school students with no access. They are 1.2 times more likely to lack access than other students.

On the opposite side of the spectrum, fewer than 25,000 students of Asian heritage lack access. Nationally, students who identify with Asian heritage comprise 5.3% of the high school population (NCES, 2017, Table 203.60). This means that they are 3.2 times less likely to lack access to college-prep coursework in their districts compared to other high school students. Figure 4.9 shows how students are disproportionately impacted by access to college prep in their traditional districts.

Figure 4.8. Students' Access to AP or IB in Their District by Racial and Ethnic Student Identity

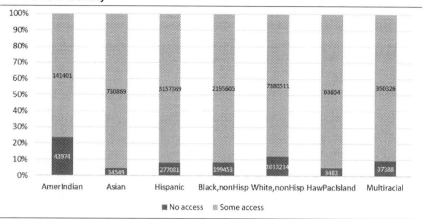

Source: Civil Rights Data Collection, 2013–14.

Figure 4.9. Drop in Access by Racial and Ethnic Identity of Students

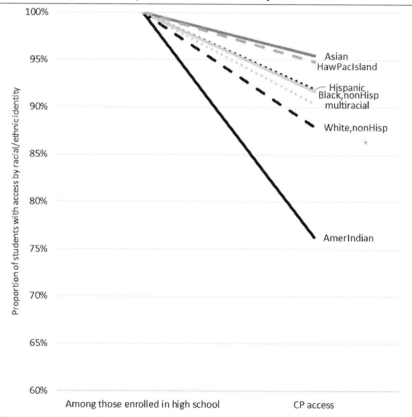

Source: Civil Rights Data Collection, 2013–14.

Figure 4.10. Students' Access to CP by Racial and Ethnic Homogeneity in District

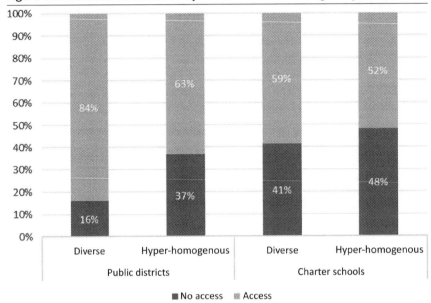

Note: "Hyper-homogeneous" is defined as a district or charter school with 90% or more of the high school students identifying as the same race or ethnicity.

Source: Civil Rights Data Collection, 2013–14.

Descriptively, we see also that hyper-homogeneous districts are less likely to have access to AP or IB (Figure 4.10). When we look further into the data using the models that consider district resources, we see that access for students attending racially or ethnically monolithic districts relates to the deficit of human and material resources common to these hyper-homogeneous districts (model 7 in online Table A4.1). This nuance of diversity does not help to explain access differences among charter schools (model 7 in online Table A4.2).

As the prior discussion of resources showed, this disproportionate impact on students is driven by the lack of access in rural districts where a larger proportion of American high school students of Native American and White, non-Hispanic heritages reside.

SUMMARY: STAGE 1 OF THE PIPELINE

To recap, 30% of the districts in the United States have no college-prep offerings. As a reminder to readers, this analysis does not count special districts that serve specialized populations—excluded are any state-run districts that serve students who are hospitalized, incarcerated, or attending exclusionary special needs schools. If we count these state-run districts, the number of American high school students who have no accessible college-prep curricula grows even larger than the 1.5 million students highlighted in this chapter. Even though trends show a rise in advanced course offerings (Donaldson, 2017; Geiser & Santelices, 2006; Judson & Hobson, 2015; Wildhagen, 2014), these findings complement those of Domina and Saldana (2012), who also found no evidence of the advanced course market saturating students' schooling experiences.

These results nuance the findings by other scholars about the differential access to AP or IB among American students. Several researchers report on the substandard access to curriculum among American Indian students at the state or regional level (Apthorp, 2016; Christenson et al., 1996; Cisneros et al., 2014; DeVoe & Darling-Churchill, 2008; Pavel & Curtin, 1997).

SPOTLIGHT STATES: HOW DOES ACCESS WORK WITHIN STATES?

The four case study states illustrate the disparities of resources across districts that do not offer any access to AP or IB courses to their high school students. Nearly half of Arizona and one-third of Michigan public school districts do not offer AP or IB. Comparatively, only one North Carolina and four Florida public districts have no access. In studying our four cases, we will first look at public district data before moving on to charter-school–specific statistics.

As these paragraphs will corroborate with the previously discussed national statistics, the racialized disparity patterns in access strongly intersect with spatial location. While these patterns do intersect, they are distinct and *not* synonymous (collinear). The racial and ethnic demographics (Figure 4.11) and residential patterns (Figure 4.12) in these four states vary widely and thus illustrate the variation of impact on students, depending on where they live.

In Arizona, lack of access severely disenfranchises students of American Indian or Alaska Native heritage; these high school students make up 20% of the students in the state with no access. American Indian or Alaska Native students in Arizona are more than two times overrepresented in districts with no AP or IB course offerings. This pattern is circumscribed in the residential patterns in Arizona, where three out of four rural districts in Arizona do not offer AP or IB courses. With that said, the rural districts with access do not differentially serve more or fewer American Indian or Alaska Native students compared to those that do not have access. In addition, the number of hyper-homogeneous American Indian or Alaska Native districts are equally likely to offer AP or IB, or not.

Figure 4.11. Spotlight States: Students' Differential Access by Racial and Ethnic Identity of Students

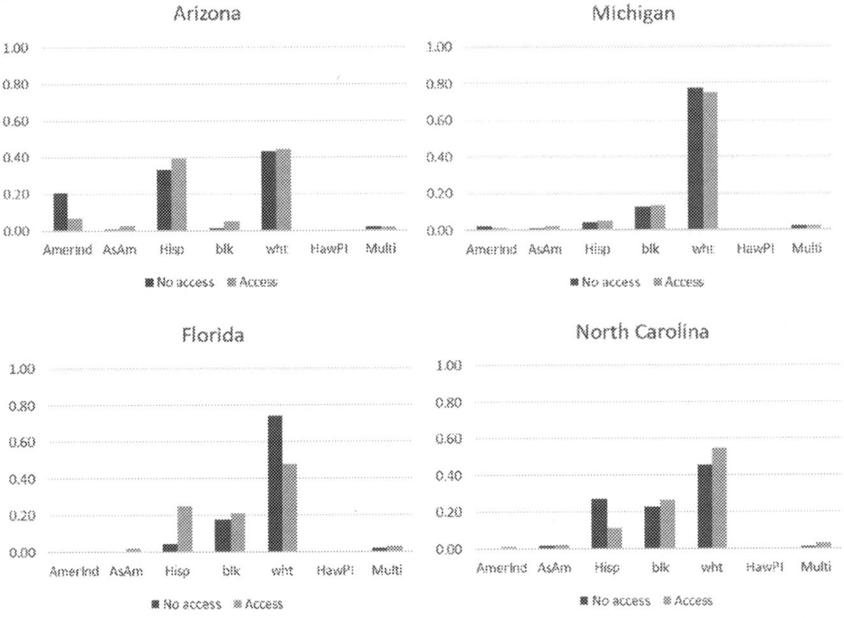

Source: Civil Rights Data Collection, 2013–14.

In North Carolina, the single district without access to AP or IB course-work abuts a national forest. This district is quite desegregated, with about a 1:1:2 student population of Hispanic, Black, non-Hispanic, and White, non-Hispanic students, respectively, attending it. This district does enroll one of the highest proportions of Hispanic students in the state (two standard deviations above the average).

In Florida, there are only four public school districts with no access to AP or IB. As the map earlier in the chapter shows, these four districts cluster in the upper north of the state. All four of the districts are rurally located and have about 1,000 students attending a single district high school. Over 80% of the attending students of three of these four districts are White, non-Hispanic. The remaining district is located near the Georgia border and reflects county desegregation orders with nearly as many Black and White, non-Hispanic students enrolled.

In Michigan, even with the new college standards embedded in the Michigan Merit Curriculum, over 30% of all districts do not offer AP or IB courses. Among rural districts, only half offer AP or IB courses. With so many Michigan districts not offering AP or IB, districts without access do not disproportionately affect students by their racial or ethnic identity.

Figure 4.12. Spotlight States: Differential Access by District Locale

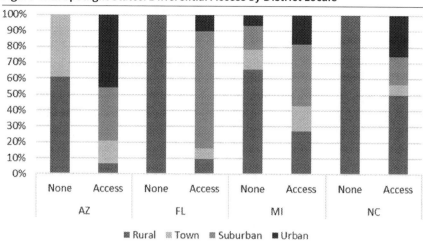

Source: Civil Rights Data Collection, 2013–14.

Table 4.1 does show, however, how the small size of Michigan districts in-duces segregated opportunities. Hyper-homogeneous districts—no matter if they serve nearly all Black, non-Hispanic or White, non-Hispanic students—make up 37% of the districts with no access. Comparatively, only 24% of Michigan districts with access are this racially isolated. Altogether, this means that the lack of access does not disproportionately impact students of certain racial or ethnic heritage in Michigan; but rather students who find themselves hyper-concentrated with other students who look like them end up with fewer opportunities to access AP or IB courses. These Michigan results parallel the hyper-homogeneity resource effects on students' access to diverse curriculum being explored by Siegel-Hawley et al. in Tennessee (2018).

When we look only at the case study data for charter organizations that do not offer AP or IB, a greater lack of access comes to the forefront. More than 75% of charter organizations in Arizona, 70% in Michigan, and 45% in North Carolina do not offer AP or IB curricula to their students. Some of these organizations may only be a single charter high school, but each state also has charter organizations that manage a collection of schools that oper-ate more like a district with a collection of schools, such as virtual schools in the state. Only Florida stands out as an outlier where these disparities in access are not prevalent.

Together, these four states show how the locale intersects with most of the racial and ethnic patterns of access. Rural students severely lack access, as Figure 4.12 shows. The few districts without access in Florida and North Carolina are rural. In Arizona, every district without access is either rural or

Table 4.1. Spotlight States: Differences Between District Access to College Prep

	Arizona		Florida		Michigan		North Carolina	
	No access	Access	No access	Access	No access	Access	No access	Access
District size/locale								
Rural	61%	6%	100%	10%	66%	27%	100%	50%
Town	39%	15%	0%	7%	13%	16%	0%	7%
Suburban	0%	33%	0%	73%	15%	39%	0%	17%
Urban	0%	46%	0%	10%	7%	18%	0%	26%
Average size of district	330	9481	995	36583	534	2291	1251	10755
Average # high schools	1.3	6.4	3.0	39.2	1.8	3.5	3.0	11.4
<30 secondary certified teachers	97%	20%	0%	1%	78%	23%	100%	5%
Student demographics								
American Indian or Alaska Native	20%	7%	1%	0%	2%	1%	0%	1%
Asian	1%	3%	0%	2%	1%	2%	2%	2%
Hispanic	33%	39%	5%	25%	5%	5%	27%	11%
Black, non-Hispanic	1%	5%	18%	21%	13%	14%	23%	27%
White, non-Hispanic	43%	44%	75%	48%	77%	75%	46%	55%
Hawaiian/Pac Islander	0%	0%	0%	0%	0%	0%	0%	0%
Multiracial	2%	2%	2%	3%	2%	2%	2%	3%
Hyper-homogenous district	17%	4%	0%	0%	37%	24%	0%	2%
Title1 district	86%	98%	89%	75%	78%	43%	100%	80%

Note: Boldface font indicates $p < .05$ on t-test difference of two-sample means. No t-test can run for North Carolina since the $n = 1$ for "no access."

Source: Civil Rights Data Collection, 2013–14.

town. Michigan is the only spotlight state where students residing in suburban or urban areas are not immune to lack of access.

Given the impact of locale, it is not surprising to see in Table 4.1 that districts without access serve significantly smaller student populations. Locale reverberates in human resource availability as well. Table 4.1 shows the large gaps in the secondary-certified teacher pool in Arizona, Michigan, and North Carolina.[6] For Arizona and Michigan, where there are substantial numbers of districts without access, it is common to have small pools of certified teachers to draw upon to teach these courses.

Table 4.1 also shows the more nuanced story of the role of poverty in these numbers. The majority of the districts with no access are highly impoverished and receive districtwide Title I funding.[7] Yet it is only in Michigan that a clear difference in disparity relates to the districts' student income status.

The spotlight states' patterns repeat the overall, general pattern that U.S. districts without college prep are substantially more rural, smaller than

Figure 4.13. Achievement Score Distribution Differences Between Districts With or Without AP and IB Access

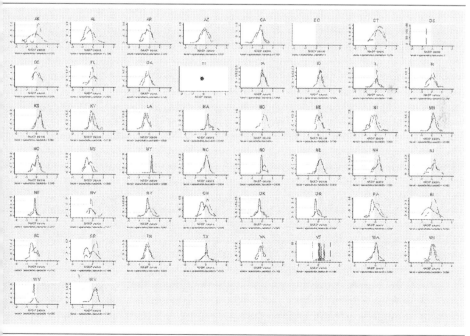

A larger and more detailed version of this figure is available in the online appendix, available for free at https://www.tcpress.com/the-fractured-college-prep-pipeline-9780807765029

the other districts in the state, and employ far fewer teachers who are certified to teach secondary-education–specific subjects.

In addition, Figure 4.13 shows how the ability theory counterargument holds little weight. There is no measurable difference in achievement scores between districts with or without access in Arizona, Florida, North Carolina, or 41 other states and the District of Columbia.[8] Only Michigan and four other states (New York, Ohio, Pennsylvania, South Dakota) show significantly lower average student achievement in districts without access compared to those with access. These states (except South Dakota) are highlighted by Fahle and Reardon (2017) as states with particularly wide gaps of achievement between districts. In particular, Fahle and Reardon (2017) link these district achievement disparities to high levels of gaps in learning opportunities linked to White-Black residential as well as economic segregation.

These findings show that, overwhelmingly, the disproportionate access is not a structural function of race, ethnicity, poverty, or academic abilities,[9] but rather one of spatial spread. However, the residential patterns of these four states cannot be understated. All four of these states have serious social issues regarding historical oppression, housing segregation, racial gerrymandering, and gentrification that helped create these spatial divides. These statewide racial issues directly link to the spatial patterns in these states, which then directly impact students' access to AP and IB high school coursework and the associated college opportunities.

CONCLUSION

The results in this chapter expand the call for attention to a national outcry and buttress the differential access explanation to include a spatial component (Curran & Kitchin, 2019). This spatial aspect also reinforces work by Gagnon and Mattingly, who discuss the inadequate human resources in farming and ranching communities (2016) that experience dead spots for college recruiting (Crain, 2018; Pappano, 2017).

These results call for social policies to alleviate these issues, which pervade the educational system and the subsequent life chances of children. Disparate access depending on where a student lives is not a social accident. These patterns of residence are deeply embedded in the history of discrimination in the United States—from corralling Indigenous Peoples to the United States to desolate reservation lands to drawing school district lines to hyper-segregate student populations. Importantly, expanding school choice is no solution here because open enrollment rarely crosses district boundaries, and charter schools are less likely to spend resources on college-prep curricula.

COMING UP NEXT

The next chapter moves to the second stage of the pipeline to understand the association of resources with participation in these courses. When we move to this section of the puzzle to understand counterfeit opportunities to learn, the models exclude the more than 3,000 districts with no access from the next chapter's discussion. It stands to reason, then, that the resources associated with lack of any access to college-prep curriculum are likely different than the resources that impact the participation rates in college-prep courses among districts that offer it.

CHAPTER 5

In the Pipeline

Participating in AP and IB Courses

The prior chapter established that despite the "college for all" expectations pervading the nation, a fair number of districts and charter schools do not offer any AP or IB opportunities to 10% of the nation's high school students. This chapter turns to the second stage in the pipeline to understand the degree to which districts enroll students in these courses, what participation patterns look like, and how resources explain those patterns.

As with the prior chapter, different uses of district resources can encourage or discourage equal representation at this stage of the pipeline. However, before examining this issue, a slight detour is needed to understand how to imagine participation in college-prep (CP) courses. Looking at the data, some districts do not offer CP curricula in all of their schools (in districts where there are multiple high schools). Due to this "tracked school" design, some students may not participate in a CP course because these courses simply are not offered at their school, whereas other students may not participate despite courses available at their school. The latter is what we typically think of when we research ability tracking of students in high schools: Some students participate in the "college-prep track" courses, while others do not. The former "no college prep offered at this school" (henceforth, "no-CP school") revives an old form of tracking, which is discussed in detail next. While it may seem like these no-CP schools could be discussed in the previous chapter regarding access, the districts' ability to potentially share curricula and teacher resources among schools elevates this lack of CP coursework from an access concern to one of exclusionary nonparticipation.

To think about all of this, the evolution of tracking is briefly overviewed before discussing the national rates of CP participation and the depth of students' exposure to it. As the analysis will show, districts' organization to concentrate versus spread-out resources each result in segregated patterns of student exposure to CP curricula. This middle part of the pipeline shunts students three ways: by diverting them to a track that leads away from any exposure to any CP, leading them to a tracked school that concentrates CP exposure, or keeping all students together and selecting some out of the lunchroom to sit in CP classrooms. Equality (i.e., parity) is virtually absent at this stage in the pipeline.

BRIEF BACKGROUND ON CURRICULUM TRACKING

You the reader may be asking yourself, "Isn't separating students into different schools that offer different types of courses an antiquated, mid-20th-century form of tracking? Wasn't this practice where teachers identified students in their middle years and directed them to this high school versus that high school a thing of the mid-20th-century days in American schooling?" The answer is that the overt, policy-driven differentiated schooling never really disappeared—it simply went underground into covert policy.

This "first-generation" formal tracking between schools conjures memories of de jure schooling (Mickelson, 2001, 2005). This between-school formal tracking mirrors the German and Japanese secondary schooling systems (Kerckhoff, 2000; LeTendre et al., 2003). It functions under the social goal that the purpose of secondary school is to differentiate curriculum and pedagogical methods to prepare students for their trajectory after high school (Graham, 2005; Kerckhoff, 1993; LeTendre et al., 2003). In the United States, sending students to the old-time vocational high school instills the blue- and pink-collar soft skills of "a good alarm clock" and deference to authority, whereas the college-prep high school instills the soft skills of classic liberal arts discourse and study habits needed to keep pace in college (Collins, 1979; Kerckhoff, 1993; LeTendre et al., 2003; Tyack, 1974). Other hard skills learned in these schools, like how to use tools without cutting off your fingers in vocational schools or learning other languages with a focus on avoiding accidentally cursing out someone's mother in college-prep schools, differentiate these schools that employ this "high scope" tracking (Sørenson, 1970).

While this between-school formal tracking seemed to leave the public eye around the time of the civil rights movement, research studies show its continued prevalence in the shadows of American education. Exposés such as Rosenbaum's *Making Inequality* (1976), Metz's *Different by Design* (1986), and Kozol's *Savage Inequalities* (1991) uncovered deplorable school conditions and pushed educators and policymakers to stop this between-school curricular differentiation practice.[1] Moreover, the passage of the Individuals with Disabilities Education Act of 1990 and the accompanying Individualized Education Plans (IEPs) and the least restrictive environment requirements made it nearly illegal to limit educational opportunities to students (Office of Civil Rights, 2020). However, as the graphs in Figure 5.1 show, the exclusivity of college-prep *coursework* to some schools appears to have slipped under the public's radar, allowing a form of between-schools tracking to persist in some districts.

STUDENT ENROLLMENT IN SCHOOLS WITH AP OR IB COURSES

The graphs in Figure 5.1 show the different characteristics of schools where students are or are not exposed to CP coursework. These graphs only compare the schools in districts that offer college prep and exclude the 3,000 districts from the prior chapter that have no AP or IB course offerings anywhere. Therefore, remember: All of these students attend districts with AP or IB, so it could be possible for 100% of these students to attend schools with these classes.

Of the millions of students who attend districts or charter schools with AP or IB coursework, over 5% attend high schools with none of these curricula. This is less of an issue for students in the suburbs, as Figure 5.1 shows: A greater proportion of students in suburban schools attends schools that offer AP or IB coursework to their students compared to students attending schools in other locales.[2]

Figure 5.2 shows Hispanic, White, non-Hispanic, and students identifying with two or more races attend schools with AP or IB offerings that approximate the average rate. Asian students attend schools with AP or IB curricula at a rate higher than average, while American Indian or Alaska Native, Native Hawaiian or Other Pacific Islander, and Black, non-Hispanic students attend schools at a rate lower than average. To put it in context, the 6.5 percentage-point differential for American Indian or Alaska Native means that for every student whose heritage ties to Indigenous Peoples to the United States, 1 fewer in every 15 students attends a school that offers AP or IB compared to the rest of the district students. For students with

Figure 5.1. Locale of Students Enrolled in Schools with CP

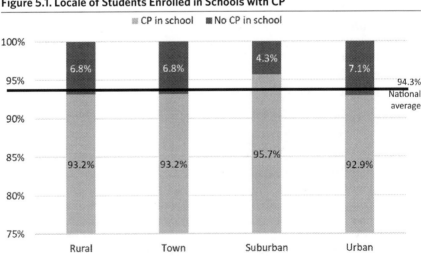

Source: Civil Rights Data Collection, 2013–14.

Figure 5.2. Racial or Ethnic Representation of Students Attending Schools with CP

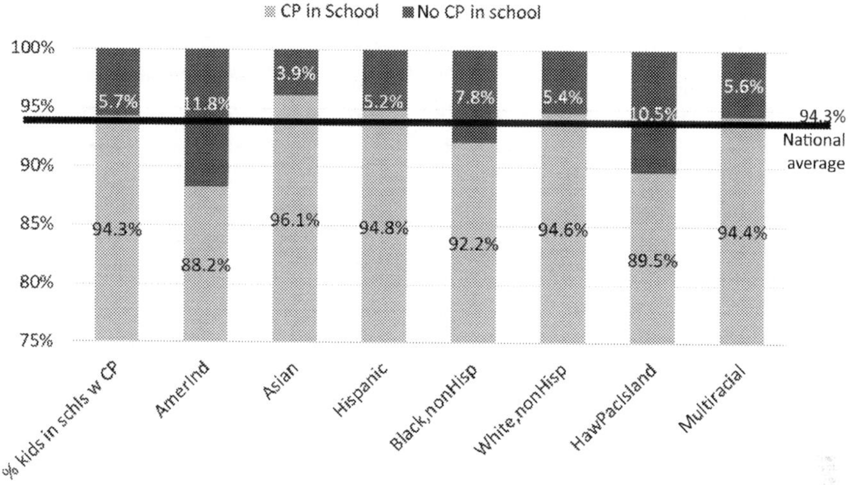

Source: Civil Rights Data Collection, 2013–14.

ancestry indigenous to Hawaii or other Pacific Islands, it is 1 fewer student for every 19 students attending a school with CP.

What does this information tell us? Nationally, Indigenous Peoples to the United States, Hawaii, and other Pacific Islands students as well as Black, non-Hispanic students often find themselves enrolled in the district schools without these curricula even though their district offers it in another school. Students affiliating with other racial or ethnic identities do not find themselves relegated to these no-CP schools. Moreover, these national differences do not appear to align with material resource markers of locale or poverty—something else seems to be going on.

This study cannot show whether these schools that do not offer AP or IB in the district serve students with lower than average achievement scores, as was the practice before IDEA laws took effect. There simply is no achievement data at the high school level to test this ability theory hypothesis.[3] As a thought experiment, however, consider the argument that if it were the case that districts were funneling their lower-achieving students into specific schools, the social justice of such a practice would raise serious ethical concerns, and IDEA would call the practice into legal question.

TRACKED-OUT: NO-CP SCHOOLS

While there is no nationally comparable information on high school–level achievement, this study can look at the question from another angle: that of resources provided to individual schools. How do the characteristics of the *school* relate to whether or not the high school offers AP or IB to its students within the district that offers these CP curricula? To test this notion, let's assess school characteristics embedded within their associated districts. This allows us to clearly identify the extent to which characteristics differ between schools with or without college-prep curricula *within the same district*. In these cases, the district resources are otherwise the same (giving us a constant), and college-prep curricula are obviously available, though puzzlingly not universal. Since this statistical model[4] requires schools to link with district resources, this model excludes charter schools since they do not have district resources to draw on. Districts with only one high school are also excluded since there is no chance of students being relegated to another school in the district. The full set of nested, multilevel models can be found in the online appendix as Table A5.1.

Results show resources matter. Figure 5.3 shows that the bigger the school, the greater the chance it will offer AP or IB curricula. Title I schools that serve substantial numbers of students experiencing poverty are 22% less likely (odds ratio coefficient, see online appendix) to offer AP or IB compared to the other schools in their district that are not Title I schools. This differentiation, however, only applies to a select number of districts that have a mix of Title I and non-Title I schools.[5]

These models also reveal that school size explains the upward skew related to Asian enrollments and Title I status explains the American Indian or Alaska Native and Native Hawaiian or Other Pacific Islander downward skews. This means that the differences in the racialized enrollment patterns of these groups of students are a function of resources in these districts and not independently associated with heritage. This is not the case for Black, non-Hispanic students. The differences in Black, non-Hispanic student enrollments in no-CP schools found in the prior pages persist and are not explained away with Title I or school size factors, but rather magnify simply due to the racial composition.

Figure 5.3 shows the real and substantial relationship between the proportion of Black, non-Hispanic students enrolled in a school and whether or not the district puts college-prep resources in that school. The 3.8 percentage-point differential for Black, non-Hispanic students means that for every 26 Black, non-Hispanic students in a district, 1 fewer Black, non-Hispanic student attends a school that offers AP or IB compared to the rest of the students in the same district. If you consider a modestly sized high school, this ends up equating a whole "regular-track" classroom of Black, non-Hispanic students who would otherwise be filling seats in a CP classroom. These models therefore show that although the CP opportunities are generally not segregating most students within multi-HS districts, these separate schools work to specifically de facto segregate Black, non-Hispanic students from schools with these CP learning opportunities.

Figure 5.3. School Characteristics Significantly Related to Whether a School Offers CP in a CP District

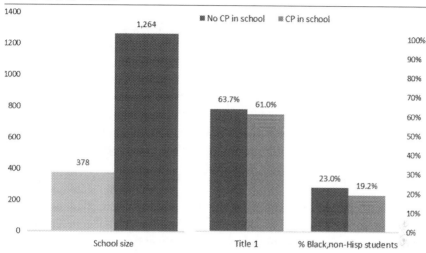

Source: Civil Rights Data Collection, 2013–14.

The results above explain that between schools in the same district, resource differences related to school size and concentrated poverty explain much of the difference regarding why some schools offer no AP or IB when they exist in a district that offers these curricula. This begs two questions: (1) Why is a correlation induced within districts regarding racial affiliation and poverty status? (2) If districts have the authority to distribute resources between their own schools, why do these material differences persist? Theoretically, remember, these schools have access to the same teacher and community resources as other schools in their district. This discussion seems relatively quick to resolve as a monetary equality issue.

This analysis reveals a glaring race-based inequality: Schools with no college-prep curricula serve substantially greater proportions of Black, non-Hispanic students than the other schools in the same district. We know from the research of Gary Orfield and the UCLA Civil Rights Project (Frankenberg & Orfield, 2012; Orfield, 2001; Orfield & Eaton, 1996; Orfield & Yun, 1999) and others (Clotfelter, 2004; Phillips & Chin, 2004) that between-school segregation still occurs in the post–Jim Crow southern schools. From Renzulli and Roscigno (2005) and others (Bifulco & Ladd, 2008; Lauen, 2007; Renzulli & Evans, 2005), we know that within-district school choice is additionally resegregating schools. These results point a policy laser on the educational opportunity consequences incurred by Black, non-Hispanic students in districts where intradistrict segregation occurs using between-school tracking. It sounds eerily similar to that of the Jim Crow era.

AP AND IB PARTICIPATION IN THE UNITED STATES

In addition to being flushed out of the pipeline by attending a school with no college-prep offerings, students can also leak out of the pipeline at this stage if they do not register for any of the AP or IB courses in their school. Which students register for these classes? How do these students compare to their peers who do not participate in any of their school's AP or IB courses?

Nationally, 16% of high school students participate in at least one AP or IB course. Figure 5.4 represents students registered in AP or IB classes among their peers who identify within the same racial or ethnic group. These percentages are averaged across districts, which allows us to think about what a college-prep classroom looks like in the "average" American school district. As a point of reference, we would expect that a portion of high school students are too early in their coursework to participate in AP or IB. If we think, at a minimum, that only seniors are allowed to register for AP courses, and every senior participated in at least one AP course, then we would expect 25% of the students to participate and 75% not to participate in a typical grade 9–12 high school. Of course, it would not likely be the case that all seniors would enroll in an AP course or that juniors or even sophomores would be wholly excluded. This example is shared as a way to prime the expectations for what the graphic displays.

Figure 5.4. Student Participation Rates in AP or IB Courses in Traditional Public School Districts

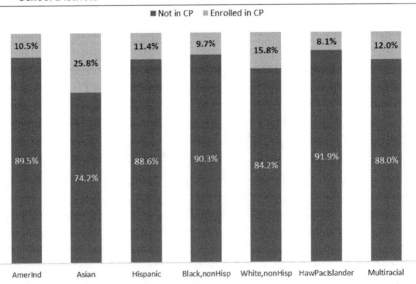

Note: *n* = 7,403 CP districts.

Source: Civil Rights Data Collection, 2013–14.

Why does it matter to represent the statistics so that one district equals one point in the dataset? Imagine, instead, if we simply provided the percent of Native Hawaiian or Other Pacific Islander students in college-prep courses in the United States. The analysis would have to artificially impute these students into the "average" classroom across the United States where they would lose their voice in the classroom as "less than one" student. Instead, data presented at the district level allow a strong voice to the students in the Hawaiian district and represent 1 in 3 students in the classroom. The average of this district with college-prep enrollments in California, Washington, and other districts with substantial populations of these students can then be compared. Thus, this study compares the average percentage of students in CP classrooms across all the districts to describe the "average" classroom *when there are students attending that district* with such heritage.

Upon immediate review, we see great fluctuation in representation, from more than 25% Asian student participation to less than 10% of Black, non-Hispanic and Native Hawaiian or Other Pacific Islander students participating in CP courses. Online Appendix A5.2 shows that these national district averages vary widely by state. Fewer than 5% of American Indian or Alaska Native high school students per district sit in college-prep classrooms in Iowa, Idaho, North Dakota, South Dakota, Vermont, and West Virginia. Iowa also exposes fewer than 5% of their Hispanic high school students in their college-prep classrooms. In Louisiana, North Carolina, and South Dakota, fewer than 5% of Black, non-Hispanic students participate in college prep. Fewer than 5% of Native Hawaiian or Other Pacific Islander students sit in college-prep classrooms in districts across the United States, on average, including Hawaii. In Arizona, Mississippi, Montana, North Dakota, and South Dakota, an average of fewer than 5% of their students who identify with two or more races sit in college-prep classrooms.

Granted, Iowa, North Dakota, and South Dakota simply expose few students in AP or IB in general, but the aforementioned students are still underrepresented compared to their other peers. No state, even Iowa, North Dakota, and South Dakota, average a participation rate below 5% among their Asian student population. Ten states exceed a 30% participation average among Asian students. No other group surpasses 30% representation in any state. Lastly, except for these three states, no state averages a district participation rate under 10% among its White, non-Hispanic student population. Thus, even in states with overall low participation rates, racialized disparities exist among which students get to sit in the exclusive CP classroom seats.

Do stereotypes appear to influence which students get tracked into AP or IB courses while others are steered away from these classes? These data cannot uncover biases that may be influencing course participation recommendations from teachers, parents, or counselors, nor can these data explain if institutional racism is the cause. These data cannot get at cause or intention behind the actions. They can only show the structural patterns as social facts. Research by Steele (Perry et al., 2003; Steele & Aronson, 1995) and Jussim and Harbor (2005) explain how stereotype threat biases influence teachers' expectations and evaluations of students' abilities as well as how the halo effect biases expectations for Asian students (Tach & Farkas, 2006; Wong & Halgin, 2006). Going further, Bonilla-Silva (2019), Tyson (2011), and Lewis and Diamond (2015) describe how institutional racism conditions curricular tracking, including the impact of high school counselors' bias in course recommendations to students (Allen et al., 2008; Witenko et al., 2017).

These data can show, however, the clear patterns of district resources that link to these disproportionate educational opportunity patterns that impact students from historically marginalized backgrounds. These data show the extent to which students get flushed or leak out at this Stage 2 and how subsequent opportunities get squandered along the way for those students who remain in its trajectory.

CONCENTRATION vs. DILUTION OF CURRICULA

A central resource feature that districts use to distribute college-prep opportunities to students is to concentrate resources into single schools. This is done by funneling students into stand-alone "CP-specialty" tracked schools that house particularly large portions of their college-prep curricula in a single school.[6] Multi-HS districts commonly offer a variety of high schools: specialty schools, schools with no college prep, and/or comprehensive schools with some CP course offerings for some students.[7] Figure 5.5 shows the prevalence of these three types of schools in traditional, multi–high school (hereafter, multi-HS) public districts. The concentration/dilution of college-prep curricula in charter and single–high school districts are also presented. Charter and single–high school (hereafter, single-HS) districts are teased apart from the multi-HS districts in the first column because no between-school tracking option can exist; these schools house all their students in either a specialty or a comprehensive high school.

The map in Figure 5.6 shows the concentration/dilution across the nation's districts. Completely black areas identify where the specialty school is the only option for students to participate in college prep in multi-HS districts and the other schools in the district do not offer any AP or IB courses. The darker the gradient of gray, the higher the proportion of high school students in the district participating in AP or IB courses. Single-HS districts can only be a gradient of gray. Districts that offer no college prep at all (as discussed in Chapter 4) remain as the white space on the map. The map shows most districts as light gray, indicating low participation. A smaller cluster of higher participation in darker gray occurs in Florida and along the

Figure 5.5. Schools with Concentrated, Comprehensive, or No AP or IB Offerings

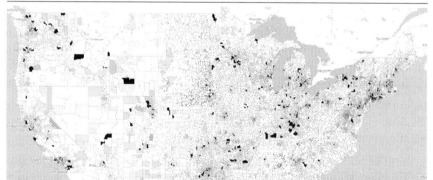

Chart data — All high school districts: 21.0% CP specialty school, 65.9% CP in school, 13.1% No CP in school. Single-high school districts: 8.3% CP specialty school, 91.7% CP in school. Charter high schools: 25.1% CP specialty school, 74.9% CP in school.

Legend: ■ No CP in school   ▩ CP in school   ▨ CP specialty school

Source: Civil Rights Data Collection, 2013–14.

Figure 5.6. Concentration of AP and IB Courses Available to Students in Traditional Public School Districts

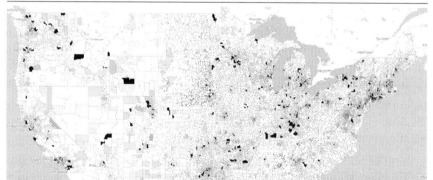

Note: Neither Hawaii nor Alaska has only specialty districts. Hawaii averages 10% of high school students in AP or IB courses in its district. Alaska districts range from 1% to 20% of high school students in AP or IB courses among its 15 districts that offer college prep (mean = 10%, s.d. 1.4%). Secondary-only districts are excluded from the map illustration.

A larger and more detailed version of this map is available in the online appendix, available at https://www.tcpress.com/the-fractured-college-prep-pipeline-9780807765029

Figure 5.7. Significant Characteristic Differences for Concentrated, Comprehensive, or No-CP Schools Within CP Districts

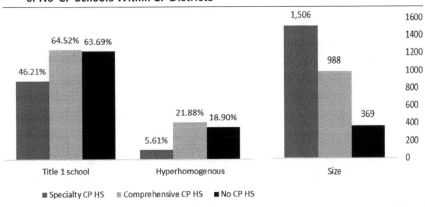

Source: Civil Rights Data Collection, 2013–14.

Northeast coast. Specialty school as the only option scatters throughout the continental United States.

How are these specialty schools resourced? To start, 1 in 12 single-HS districts specialize in college-prep curriculum for all their students. These are overwhelmingly suburban districts. Figure 5.7 shows that specialty high schools are far less impoverished, far less hyper-homogeneous (aka more diverse), and are much larger than the comprehensive or no-CP schools. Regarding these resources, the concentrated no-CP schools are not much different than the comprehensive high schools, other than serving fewer students.[8]

INSIDE THE CLASSROOMS

What does the AP or IB classroom look like compared to the students in the lunchroom in these different types of schools? Figure 5.8 presents a set of stacked bar graphs to show how the overall school body looks altogether in the lunchroom compared to who sits in the AP and IB classrooms. To compare apples to apples, these graphs only compare schools in districts with a CP-specialty school plus at least one other high school option.[9]

As a benchmark, the first column shows the diversity of the student population in all eligible, multi-HS districts. Overall, approximately 37% of the students identify as White, non-Hispanic, 24% as Black, non-Hispanic, 28% as Hispanic, 7% as Asian, 2.5% as two or more races, less than 1% as American Indian or Alaska Native, and less than 1% as Hawaiian or Other Pacific Islander. Comparatively, specialty schools overenroll White, non-Hispanic and Asian students, while comprehensive schools overenroll

Figure 5.8. Comparing the Lunchroom to the CP Classroom in Schools

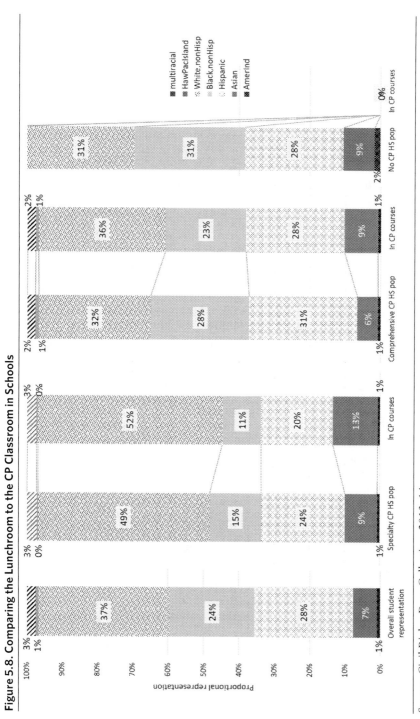

Source: Civil Rights Data Collection, 2013–14.

Black, Hispanic, and two or more race students. Schools with no CP un-derenroll White, non-Hispanic students and overenroll Asian, Black, non-Hispanic, and American Indian or Alaska Native students compared to the average student population in these districts.

The disparity between the lunchroom and the CP classroom student population follows a similar pattern whether students attend a specialty or comprehensive high school: White, non-Hispanic and Asian students dis-proportionately participate in CP courses, while Black, non-Hispanic and Hispanic students are underrepresented. Due to the diversion of some stu-dents in the pipeline to the schools with no CP, a spillover occurs that creates greater underrepresentation in specialty schools and greater overrepresenta-tion in comprehensive schools. Let's not gloss over the paradoxical nature of this state of affairs: underrepresentation *can be greatest in specialty schools* even though there is such a wide availability of AP and IB seats available. These national results differ from Southworth and Mickelson's study (2007) that found greater equality in CP track assignment in racially balanced schools, but this may speak to the finding of Kelly and Price (2011) that fewer track options (i.e., lower selectivity) is more common in racially het-erogeneous North Carolina high schools. These findings underscore prior national results linking particularly high rates of African American disparity in integrated schools (Kelly, 2009).

> This argument of representation is basic and does not even touch on the issue of equity (see Gutiérrez & Jaramillo [2006] for discussion). The reason why this study focuses on representation is that it is the most minimal standard of educa-tional opportunity codified in *Brown v. Board of Education.* Efforts to work on equity are based on the notion that students have equal opportunity as a foundation. This study, however, shows that such an equality simply does not exist for CP coursework, hence the focus on representation.

TRACKED-IN: CP-SPECIALTY SCHOOLS

Now that we have established that students' participation routes in the CP pipeline differ by school design, let's return to the resource question: To what extent do resources explain when districts institute a design where stu-dents can attend a school specializing in college-preparation coursework? The details from these district-level models can be found at Table A5.3 in the online appendix. The resources related to the establishment of a CP-specialty high school look basically the same whether a district has multiple or only one high school. Multi-HS districts just reallocate resources more quickly than single-HS districts.

Specialty schools pop up less often as the proportion of White, non-Hispanic student population rises. That is, the district is slower to establish a specialty school as the proportion of White, non-Hispanic students in the district rises. Instead, comprehensive high school designs are used to provide all students available CP courses. The reverse is also true: Districts more quickly establish CP-specialty schools as the proportion of White, non-Hispanic students become less of the majority.

Amidst the variation in district populations, there is a break point: Hyper-homogeneous districts that enroll a super-majority of students identifying as the same race or ethnicity are 1.75 times more likely to establish a CP-specialty school in a multi-HS district. This means that these districts concentrate CP curricula into a specialty school among students who overwhelmingly share similar racial or ethnic heritage. Although this study cannot test the hypothesis with these data, this seems to point to Lucas's notion of effectively maintained inequality, where groups subdivide status when the group otherwise looks average as a whole (Lucas, 2001). It also echoes Attewell's study (2001) about contested classroom spots among socioeconomically elite groups.

Thinking of locale, there is no appreciable difference in suburban and urban districts as to whether or not they establish CP-specialty schools. Rural districts, on the other hand, are less likely to establish CP-specialty schools. The size of the high school population in the district only matters for multi-HS districts: Bigger district populations increase the chance of specialty schools in multi-HS districts.

Limited teacher resources relate to the specialty school structural design. When districts have few secondary-certified teachers on their payroll, they appear to concentrate these experts to these tracked specialty schools. Multi-HS districts are over 5.3 times more likely to establish a CP-specialty school design if they have limited (less than 30) secondary-certified teachers on their district roster. Single-HS districts and charters, by contrast, adopt a specialty CP concentration at a three times slower rate with this teacher roster size. When multi-HS districts have large rosters (more than 100) of secondary-certified teachers, there is a lower chance of adopting the CP-specialty school structure.

The patterns for the single-HS districts are interesting to compare to the patterns of the charter schools since we could think of them as allocating and using resources with similar organizational procedures because neither has to split resources with another high school. The resources matter much less to charter schools than to single-HS districts, however. For both, locale does not matter, nor do hyper-homogeneous student populations. The White, non-Hispanic population and the teacher resources work similarly in both contexts. However, charter schools receiving Title I funding act more like multi-HS districts where they are less likely to establish CP as a specialty in their charter school if a substantial number of their students are experiencing poverty.

By now you are likely asking yourself how academic ability plays into all of this: How much do the 8th-grade test scores of the students influence whether or not districts establish a CP-specialty school? Does the variation in students' abilities within a district create a demand for the pull-out tracking that specialty schools can provide to those high-testing students? To answer the last question first, the short answer is that there is a slight influence of variation on the establishment of specialty schools in multi-HS districts. It is slight because the model shows that there is a 9% greater chance to establish a specialty school among districts that average a standard deviation twice as wide as the average district. In statistics we call this a "significant but unsubstantial" difference. It's mentioned for the comprehensiveness of the discussion, but you can understand why it is hardly worth a mention.

The graphs show how the 8th-grade district test scores interact with locale and Title I resources. In multi-HS districts, Figure 5.9 shows how resource-rich districts—those in the suburbs and where most of the students do not receive subsidized lunch funding—more quickly adopt a specialty school among their multiple high schools than the other districts.

Although the models in Table A5.3 column 1 (see online Appendix) show that rural and town multi-HS districts adopt specialty schools less quickly than urban multi-HS districts, Figure 5.9 shows how this is mostly tied to their relationship with standardized test scores. There is little difference in adopting the CP-specialty school design in rural, town, urban, or Title I multi-HS

Figure 5.9. Predicted Probability of Adopting a CP-Specialty School in Multi-HS Districts

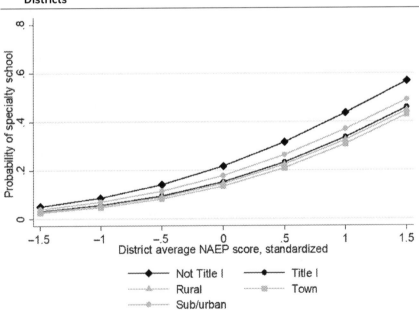

Source: Civil Rights Data Collection, 2013–14.

districts. For these districts, there is a 35% greater chance that their district will adopt a CP-specialty school if their students average a whole standard deviation higher average score in 8th grade compared to the national average.

Figure 5.10 shows the same pattern does not occur in single-HS districts. In these districts, Title I funding boosts the pace of converting their single high school to a CP-heavy curricula. The pace is slower in rural single-HS districts. Despite the slower likelihood of conversion, the curve of the line shows that the pace is equivalent to the multi-HS district average: There is a 35% greater chance that a rural single-HS district will convert to a CP-specialty curricula if their students average a whole standard deviation higher average score in 8th grade compared to the national average. The chance of CP-specialty curricula adoption in other locales and Title I single-HS districts based on the standardized test score average is lower to start but then once students average a mean that is 0.5 standard deviation higher than the national average, the chance of conversion to CP-heavy curricula is high. Baseline 8th-grade achievement strongly relates to adopting a CP-heavy curricula in these single-HS districts.

Figure 5.11 shows quite a flat adoption model for charter schools. Standardized test scores are only half as influential to adopting a CP-specialty

Figure 5.10. Predicted Probability of Adopting a CP-Specialty Curricula in Single-HS Districts

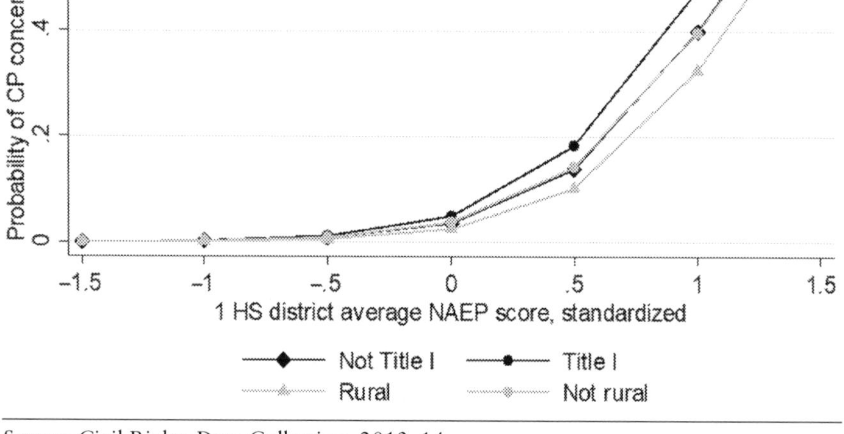

Source: Civil Rights Data Collection, 2013–14.

curricula in charter schools as compared to multi-HS districts (see also columns 1 and 3 online in Table A5.3). Locale resources do not differentiate adoption. Title I charter schools are 40% slower to adopt a CP-specialty curricula than non-Title I charter schools. Although this may seem more promising on the surface since resources do not predicate the adoption of CP-heavy curricula, Chapter 6 will show how charter schools' CP instruction fails their students based on these schools' abysmal AP pass rates.

The physical structure of school buildings matters. How resources impact structural decisions about adopting a CP-specialty school depends on whether the district has multiple school buildings or only one; charter status also plays a role in this equation. Multi-HS districts and charter schools are quick to hoard resources when standardized test score averages are low, while single-HS districts do not convert until test scores reach an above-average threshold and then quickly convert the whole high school to a heavy CP focus.

The adoption of a CP-specialty school in high-scoring multi-HS districts may seem counterintuitive because the between-schools tracking notion assumes that districts would siphon off their few high-scoring students to the specialty school while the others remain in the comprehensive high schools. This echoes research that shows track structures simply slide upward to

Figure 5.11. Predicted Probability of Adopting a CP-Specialty Curricula in Charter Schools

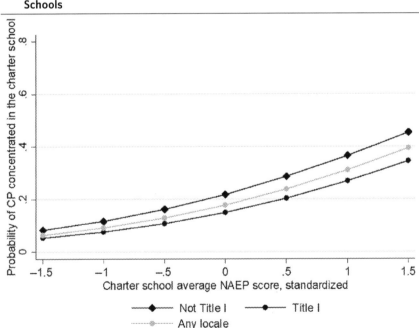

Source: Civil Rights Data Collection, 2013–14.

maintain a hierarchy—just now at a more advanced level—among opportunities to learn (Domina & Saldana, 2012; Domina et al., 2016; Kelly & Price, 2011). However, Lucas's EMI theory (1999) predicts this exact behavior: When everyone begins to achieve above average, then motivation commences to distinguish among the elite. In this case, specialty schools function to distinguish quality among a commodity that is universal.

CONCENTRATION vs. DILUTION: IMPACT ON PARTICIPATION RATES

The majority of schools do not specialize in CP but rather offer AP or IB curricula among their regular courses. In a comprehensive high school, students choose their schedules based on a published Academic Bulletin of courses and participate according to their likes, their interests, or their teacher, parent, or school counselor recommendations.[10] This section looks at how the level of student participation in AP or IB varies by their districts' resources.

Some schools, like specialty schools, can offer many seats in AP or IB courses, so that more students can take these classes. Other schools may offer a wide range of AP or IB courses but only have enough resources to serve one classroom per course. This design often turns into the honors track group of students participating in the same string of classes, leaving other students with no access to them. Other schools may offer fewer choices of courses but serve many classrooms of students per course, and so more students get exposed to some AP or IB. These designs determine who can participate in AP or IB courses due to the allocation of seats in the classrooms that determine the proportion of a cohort with the opportunity to learn ("track inclusiveness" according to Sørenson [1970]). Table A5.3 (see online Appendix) provides the output of the estimates[11] summarized in the following paragraphs.

Districts with specialty schools fill one more AP or IB classroom for every 150 high schoolers in the district. CP participation rates are lower if students attend rural or township districts. Community poverty compounds low participation; participation rates are additionally lower if all district schools receive Title I to supplement low incomes in the community.

Participation rates also relate to human resource limits: Districts with less than 30 secondary teachers on the roster do not offer as many CP course seats as other districts. On the flip side, suburban districts and districts with large teacher rosters of more than 100 secondary-certified teachers associate with greater numbers of high school students in CP seats.

The impact of these resources is stable whether we look at resources in isolation or together. What this means is that there is no substitution of one resource for another—they each work as independent determinants of participation rates of high school students in CP courses.[12] For example, the impact of locale is not supplanted by Title I status.

Once the human and material resources are accounted for, few student body compositions substantially relate to the proportion of CP course seats offered in a district, supporting prior research by Kelly (2004). Bias does still correlate with two student groups: The greater the proportion of Asian students attending the district corresponds with higher participation rates in AP or IB courses, while it corresponds with lower rates when the proportion of Native Hawaiian or Other Pacific Islander students attending the district increases.

Interestingly, the standardized test scores that mattered quite a bit in determining the specialty school structure appear to have little or no relationship to the participation rates of students taking CP courses. Districts where students average a whole standard deviation higher score (which is a lot higher) only add one more classroom of AP or IB for every 400 high school students in the district.[13] This paltry difference is another instance of "significant but not very substantial" impact.

The model for charter schools works similarly. Students attending Title I charter schools have lower CP participation rates. Charter schools with large teacher rosters average higher participation rates of students in AP or IB. Charter schools that specialize in CP curricula look a lot like traditional public districts with another AP or IB classroom filled with students for every 160 high schoolers at the charter school. A notable difference is that there exists a slight bias to place more students in CP seats in charter schools as the proportion of Black, non-Hispanic students rises.

It is important to remember that these models account for the state differences in graduation requirements: The differences in the graduation standards between states like New York and Hawaii are not driving these results about why some districts teach greater or lesser amounts of CP curricula.

SUMMARY: STAGE 2 OF THE PIPELINE

To summarize, the prior chapter addressed access to opportunities, while this chapter addressed the hypotheses about resources shaping the classroom experiences of students, as Figure 5.12 highlights in the boxed area.

These analyses showed how these CP course offerings provide substantial opportunities to some students while not to others. Some districts relegate students to schools that offer no AP or IB, while others in their district get the chance to take these courses. The between-schools tracking of Black, non-Hispanic students to no-CP schools is especially prevalent, whereas CP-specialty schools occur more often among hyper-segregated districts or in districts with smaller White, non-Hispanic populations.

This chapter also showed how human resources of the number of certified teachers impacts CP participation rates. Students who attend poorly resourced schools with few secondary-certified teachers get less exposure

Figure 5.12. Resource Hypotheses Explaining Variation in Stage 2

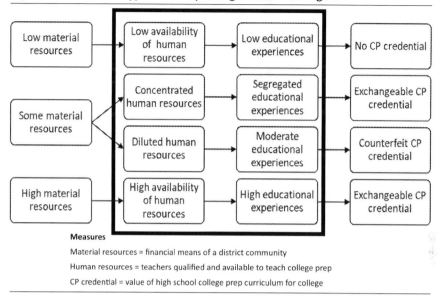

Measures

Material resources = financial means of a district community

Human resources = teachers qualified and available to teach college prep

CP credential = value of high school college prep curriculum for college

to CP courses simply because capacity is limited. Moreover, students in districts with less community wealth, such as those attending Title I districts or those residing in rural areas or small towns, receive fewer experiences to participate in CP.

The 8th-grade achievement scores do substantially relate to the organizational decision to adopt a design that separates some students from the rest of the district using a between-schools, formal tracking design. However, students' average 8th-grade ability levels in districts do little to shape the level of CP exposure for their students—and this varies, depending on which state students reside in, as Figure 5.13 shows. The 8th-grade achievement scores of students negligibly impact the rates of student exposure to CP coursework in the district or charter schools. These results echo Hallinan and Sørenson (1983), who found students fit into predefined, closed-position instructional groups rather than schools shaping their curricular organization to the students' abilities.

Once these tracked schools are accounted for, participation rates within schools follow the longtime pattern: White, non-Hispanic and Pan-Asian students occupy more college-prep seats in classrooms than their peers. Some researchers explain this as a form of opportunity hoarding (Kelly & Price, 2011), while others explain it as a social–psychological consequence of the Pygmalion effect (Jussim & Harbor, 2005; Rosenthal & Jacobson, 1968; Rosenholtz & Rosenholtz, 1981; Tyson, 2011; Vanfossen et al., 1987) or the Matthew effect (Kerckhoff & Glennie, 1999; Lewis &

Figure 5.13. Correlation of Districts' Average 8th-Grade Test Scores with CP Participation Rates

A larger and more detailed version of this figure is available in the online appendix, available for free at https://www.tcpress.com/the-fractured-college-prep-pipeline -9780807765029

Diamond, 2015; Rigney, 2010; Tyson, 2011) accumulated from teachers' expectations shaping students' educational trajectories. No matter the reason, the social fact remains that decades of racialized curriculum tracking assignments persist in the advanced course-taking arena, as so many other scholars have documented (Lewis & Diamond, 2015; Lucas & Berends, 2002; Mickelson, 2015; Mickelson & Everett, 2008; Phillips & Chin, 2004; Tyson, 2011).

Before moving on to the final, analytic chapter, which investigates the successes of students in these courses, I next discuss how CP participation looks and operates in the four spotlight states.

SPOTLIGHT STATES: HOW DOES PARTICIPATION WORK WITHIN STATES?

The four case study states demonstrate a variety of tracked schools as well as a range of racial or ethnic disparities in student participation in CP courses. The design of no-CP schools is uncommon in Arizona, with only 7% of their high schools following this formal tracked school design. More than 11% of Michigan schools have this design, however. Comparatively, 1 in 5 high schools in Florida (19%) and North Carolina (20%) offer no AP or IB in schools nested in districts with these curricular offerings.[14]

On the other side of tracked schools, Florida does not have any CP-specialty high schools. Even though there is a strong presence of IB in Florida, this IB curriculum is embedded in comprehensive high school designs. Michigan's districts with CP-specialty schools neighbor districts where AP offerings occur ubiquitously in every high school. In comparison, Arizona districts that only offer CP through a specialty school design typically abut districts with no access to CP curriculum. North Carolina has only one district where all high school students attend high schools that specialize in college prep. Unsurprisingly, this district is Chapel Hill-Carrboro multi-HS district located in North Carolina's flagship college city.

How are students represented in these different CP school designs? The bar graph in Figure 5.14 shows minor differences between Arizonan students who attend schools with or without CP. In the schools with CP, the participation compared to the general population mirrors the national trends: White, non-Hispanic and Asian students overrepresent in CP seats compared to their peers, who are underrepresented.

In Florida, American Indian or Alaska Native, Native Hawaiian or Other Pacific Islander, White, non-Hispanic, and students identifying with two or more races are overrepresented in schools with no AP or IB offerings. Hispanic and Black, non-Hispanic students are more often in schools that offer CP, but they sit in fewer CP classroom seats than their White, non-Hispanic and Asian schoolmates.

Figure 5.14. Spotlight States: Students' Differential Racial and Ethnic Representation in AP and IB

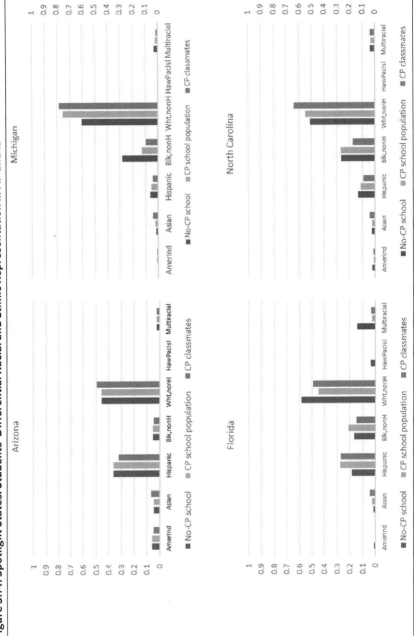

Michigan's disparities are almost entirely a black-and-white issue: 1 in 3 Black, non-Hispanic students attend tracked schools with no CP. When the 2 in 3 Black, non-Hispanic Michigander students attend schools with CP, they participate in these classes at lower rates than their schoolmates. White, non-Hispanic students make up nearly 80% of the population in schools with CP and only 60% in schools without these curricula.

North Carolina is skewed a bit more than Arizona for their schools without CP curricula. The major disparity arises with CP participation once attending schools with these courses: Hispanic and Black, non-Hispanic students are noticeably underrepresented in these classrooms while White, non-Hispanic students fill up more seats than their representation in the general school population. These results support Diette's findings (2012) that Black-White disparity looms larger when schools are less racially homogeneous.

Table 5.1 shows a complicated story of Title I funding. Arizona and North Carolina no-CP schools more often occur in districts receiving district-wide Title I funds. The same is not true for Florida, and to a lesser extent, Michigan. Schools in districtwide Title I districts in Florida and Michigan offer wider college-prep participation than non-Title I districts.

Table 5.1 also shows how school locale factors differently by state. In Arizona and Florida, the town and suburban results are similar: Fewer town schools have AP or IB, and more suburban schools have AP or IB. In Florida and North Carolina, fewer rural schools have AP or IB; the opposite is true in Michigan. Fewer urban schools in Florida and Michigan have AP or IB, but in North Carolina they have more AP or IB in their schools.

Since we know from the prior chapters that district locale distributes differently in these four states, Figure 5.15 shows the student representation in CP courses by locale among those students who attend schools with CP. Like the national averages, this graph shows how there are fewer opportunities to participate in CP courses if students reside in rural or town districts. Michigan's township students do fare better than average. Arizona students overall have lower participation unless they reside in the suburbs. Florida students have greater participation than average. Given the population distributions in these states, we know that these locales correlate with racial and ethnic residential patterns and therefore disenfranchise the learning opportunities (see Fahle & Reardon, 2017) of Native students in Arizona and Florida, rural White, non-Hispanic students in Florida, and Hispanic and Black, non-Hispanic students in Michigan and North Carolina.

Overall, these four states demonstrate the national impact of locale on curricular delivery as well as show the contextual nuance of racialized CP tracking structured in different school designs.

Table 5.1. Spotlight States: Differences Between Schools With and Without CP

	Arizona		Florida		Michigan		North Carolina	
	No-CP school	CP in school	No-CP school	CP in school	No-CP school	CP in school	No-CP school	CP in school
# schools in the state	16	197	120	522	61	459	109	427
% Charter	13%	20%	34%	12%	0%	6%	1%	6%
District size/locale								
Rural	6%	7%	18%	7%	13%	29%	59%	46%
Town	25%	13%	25%	5%	7%	16%	8%	7%
Suburban	19%	33%	19%	77%	44%	37%	14%	19%
Urban	50%	47%	50%	11%	36%	18%	19%	28%
Average district size	203.9	1447.5	287.1	1475.5	286.9	864.0	240.9	1021.3
Student demographics								
Amer Indian or Alaska Native	4%	6%	1%	0%	1%	1%	2%	1%
Asian	2%	4%	1%	3%	2%	3%	3%	2%
Hispanic	35%	36%	19%	28%	6%	5%	13%	11%
Black, non-Hispanic	4%	5%	17%	21%	28%	13%	27%	27%
White, non-Hispanic	51%	46%	58%	45%	60%	76%	51%	55%
Hawaiian or Pacific Islander	1%	0%	0%	0%	0%	0%	0%	0%
Multiracial	3%	2%	4%	3%	3%	2%	4%	3%
Hyper-homogenous district	9%	5%	15%	4%	22%	28%	1%	4%
Title1 district	100%	86%	59%	76%	40%	46%	83%	76%

Figure 5.15. Percent of Students Participating in CP Courses by Locale

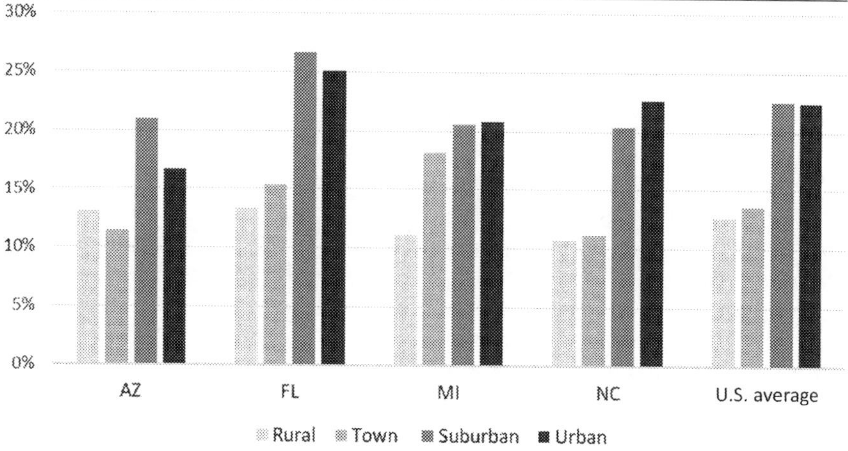

Rural Town Suburban Urban

Source: Civil Rights Data Collection, 2013–14.

CONCLUSION

It is extremely rare to find equal representations in CP participation, within districts or charter high schools. In more than 98% of schools, there is disparity between the students participating in college-prep courses and those in the general school population. This chapter clearly shows that there are ubiquitous racial and ethnic disparities in the participation numbers for college-prep courses, no matter the state or the type of school (traditional public or charter) that students attend. But the map shows how the structure of disparity varies across the American landscape.

This chapter shows how some districts' disparity occurs by excluding students using a first-generation (Mickelson, 2001, 2005) design that puts students on a track headed to a school with no CP offerings or on a track that piles on resources to students headed to the CP-specialty school. Although resource factors explain many of the racialized patterns of tracked school enrollment, the fact remains that these coexisting factors hurt certain racial groups of students—especially Indigenous Peoples to the United States, Hawaii, and other Pacific Islands and Black, non-Hispanic students—more than their other peers. This between-school tracking may be a method of keeping the "cream of the crop" at other schools by "cropping" some students to these no-CP schools (Lacireno-Paquet et al., 2002; Riel et al., 2018).

Once in schools with college-prep curricula—whether in specialty or comprehensive schools—decades-old disparities perpetuate. Diversity in specialty schools appears on the surface of school enrollment, but disparity is accentuated in the classrooms as a phenomenon that Mickelson (2001) explained 20 years ago and which she shows perpetuates resegregation in intradistrict magnet schools (Riel et al., 2018). Comprehensive schools continue to repeat historical patterns of within-school tracking.

These results rearticulate 20th-century within-schools tracking under the new auspices of AP and IB in place of the 20th-century honors track assignment. Formal between-schools tracking exclusivity of college prep in some schools and absence from other schools within the same district is likely a direct consequence of the rise of school choice within districts. Researchers such as Billingham & Hunt (2016), Posey-Maddox (2012), Riel et al. (2018), and Sattin-Bajaj & Roda (2018) demonstrate the power of the political capital of parents to demand their children's placement in specialty schools in districts over their neighborhood school. PTOs and parents advocate for priority intradistrict school choice criteria that structure procedures to favor their children over others, even in seemingly random school choice lottery systems. The political capital needed by parents to lobby for such school assignment prioritization requires cultural capital, social capital, and discretionary time that is rarely available to working-class or blue-collar parents (Lareau, 2000; Posey-Maddox, 2012; Sattin-Bajaj & Roda, 2018). Chapters 7 and 8 circle back to the social consequences of these school designs.

COMING UP NEXT

The next chapter moves to the last stage of the pipeline, where we look at the success rates of students in their college-prep courses. The AP tests indicate how well students learned the material when they participated in these courses. This chapter continues to test the argument throughout this book about the impact of district resources on whether or not students are going to earn the coveted college credit with their high school college-prep course. This next chapter includes all the districts discussed in this chapter except the handful of traditional and charter schools that only offer IB curriculum, because the CRDC does not have data on IB test results.

CHAPTER 6

The Last Stage of the Pipeline
Passing the Exams

The last chapter showed which students are excluded from participating in college prep. Students can be flushed out of the pipeline using a between-schools tracking design that shunts certain students into the district schools that lack college-prep offerings. If students attend schools with AP or IB, they can also leak out of the pipeline because they do not participate in any of these courses. This chapter turns to the last stage in the pipeline, the testing stage, to understand which students pass their exams and how they differ from those who fail to pass. This chapter introduces the newest extension of the pipeline, one that distinguishes the American 21st-century tracking from its 20th-century predecessor and creates a new counterfeit credential.

Similar to the prior pipeline stage discussed in Chapter 5, there are two ways to exit this last stage in the pipeline: Students can leak out by simply not passing their exam, or they can be flushed out if they attend districts where they are never given an exam to test their knowledge. Yes, that's right: These data show that it is a common practice for some districts to enroll students in courses and then never proctor the exam. These students never get the chance to show their level of mastery. Of course, it is this demonstration of mastery that is the exchangeable currency to earn credit for college courses (and thus put students ahead in college and possibly help them finish sooner and with less debt [Evans, 2019]). This discussion will extend into Chapter 7 to examine just how impactful this practice can be. For now, however, let's first empirically establish that this occurs before discussing consequences for students.

This chapter takes the data on which students take college-prep courses and asks: What is the quality of these courses? The question rests on the assumption that if the curricula are of high quality, then students can demonstrate their mastery on the exam. The AP exam offers an external, uniform metric to gauge this idea. Unfortunately, this dataset does not have IB exam information. However, only 101 schools out of the thousands in 2013–14 solely deliver IB curriculum and no AP, so only a minuscule number of data points are lost without this IB information.[1] With this idea about mastery knowledge, the question is: Why do students in some districts get exposed to college-prep courses of higher quality than they would if they attended other districts? Like the approach of this study, the explanation starts by looking at the differences in district resources.

To get at all of this, the issues created by the states' rights model in the United States need discussion before moving into the national trends for taking the AP exam as well as passing it. As the data will evidence, resources and school composition play outsized roles in students' exam outcomes, often as the result of troubling patterns of racial and ethnic discrimination. Students also get lost in the data reporting at this stage, and thus we cannot assess their outcomes. Getting to the final stage of the college-prep pipeline—actually getting to demonstrate college-prep mastery—should be a happy milestone for high schoolers, but as the data show, this achievement can slip away as students fail to pass the exam or fail to be offered a chance to take the exam in the first place.

U.S. HISTORY ON TESTING KNOWLEDGE: STATES' RIGHTS

Testing, testing, testing. We seem fixated on testing students to assess their knowledge in the younger grade levels (Ravitch, 2016). Federally related testing, however, is only required once during high school grades (U.S. Department of Education, 2004, 2015). Due to this dearth of high school testing, researchers have trouble comparing high schools across the nation. We hardly have an idea of how students in Arizona fare at graduation in their college readiness compared to students in North Carolina, for example. Moreover, graduation standards are determined at the state level. States also determine the grade-level learning outcomes, required courses for a high school diploma, teacher training requirements, funding allocations for schools, and all the other types of benchmarks that relate to the quality of college readiness that students receive in high school. This census of AP results is one sliver of a measure to gauge the quality of high school course-taking.

Federal regulations related to the Elementary and Secondary Education Act (ESEA) created the space for federal mandates like No Child Left Behind (NCLB) and Every Student Succeeds Act (ESSA). These federal laws mandate testing in the same way that the federal highway commission encourages highway regulations: These laws set up sanctions if states do not follow the federal recommendations. In the case of the highway commission, if states do not adopt the 0.08 BAC blood alcohol level for drinking and driving, then the federal government retracts federal highway funding to that state (Mid-America Research Institute, 2001). Why does the system work this way? In the United States, driving regulations are a states' rights issue and not under the jurisdiction of the federal government (Mid-America Research Institute, 2001). The same is true for schooling: It is a states' rights issue mandated by state constitutions (Chermerinsky, 2002;

Clotfelter, 2004; Smith & Crosby, 2008). Federal rights such as the civil rights protected in the U.S. Constitution supersede state jurisdiction, which is how state regulations such as segregated schooling in *Brown v. Board of Education* became federal issues.

The implication from schooling as a state's jurisdiction is that the federal government can use some budget power, such as to retract funding for school lunch programs, special education, and other federally funded programs, to encourage publicly funded districts and charter schools to follow federal guidelines such as administering annual tests of knowledge to their students (Clotfelter, 2004; Ravitch, 2016; USDOE, 2020b). This round-about regulatory power is why the United States is one of the few industrialized nations that does not have a national test to compare students (OECD, 2015). It also explains how graduation and dropout rates vary widely throughout the United States and why racial and ethnic disparities in education strongly tie to state histories.[2]

State-level control of education complicates comparing the achievement test scores of American students. Most studies about tested achievement scores restrict their analysis to within a state or administer their own achievement tests to the students in their study. The latter is how the National Center for Education Statistics typically runs their studies: They administer their own tests to students to enter into the database so that the students' scores are measured on the same instrument. Alternatively, some studies use students' transcripts where they can match the course name to the course grades and estimate students' mastery over the material typically taught in that course (An, 2013a, 2013b; Austin, 2020; Minor, 2015; Minor et al., 2015). AP exam results provide a nationally comparable measure of high school student learning for a certain academic subgroup of high school students.

AP EXAMS

The analysis in this chapter fills a longstanding absence in U.S. education research to account for the variation in the quality of curricula across American high schools (Coleman, 1990; Gamoran et al., 2000; Lucas, 2001). While it cannot capture the quality of all high school curricula, it can capture it for advanced course-taking to start the conversation on quality differences between schools.

Until now, grades linked to course descriptions from administrative transcript records in nationally representative sample-based datasets have been the best proxies for assessing the quality of curriculum since the U.S. state-based education system leaves little room for any type of national assessment of curriculum or its quality.[3] This chapter provides a more proximate and valid measure of quality because it uses the College Board's

Advanced Placement exams to compare the learning outcomes of students participating in the same classes across the nation.[4] Further, these tests are evaluated by the external College Board organization, and thus there is no federal sanction threat to pressure internal evaluators in state education offices to politically spin these scores.

The map in Figure 6.1 clearly shows the different patterns by state around AP testing. As with the other maps, the blank areas are districts that have already been excluded from the analysis because they do not offer any college-prep courses in their district. The darker the gray, the greater the proportion of students who did not pass any of their AP exams. The lighter the gray, the lower the failure rates. It's easy to see that many districts in the heartland, as demonstrated by states like Montana, Kansas, and Nebraska, have very low failure rates. On the other hand, the cluster of darker gray in the Appalachian region, Arkansas, and Florida quickly draws attention to high rates of students not passing their AP exams. These gradients of gray explain this final way students leak out of the college-prep pipeline: They do not pass their exams to demonstrate their mastery to prospective colleges. The black areas on the map identify where students have no opportunity to show mastery because no exam was proctored to them. They've taken the courses, done the work, but it doesn't count for college credit.

Figure 6.1. Concentration of Failing to Pass AP Exams in Traditional School Districts

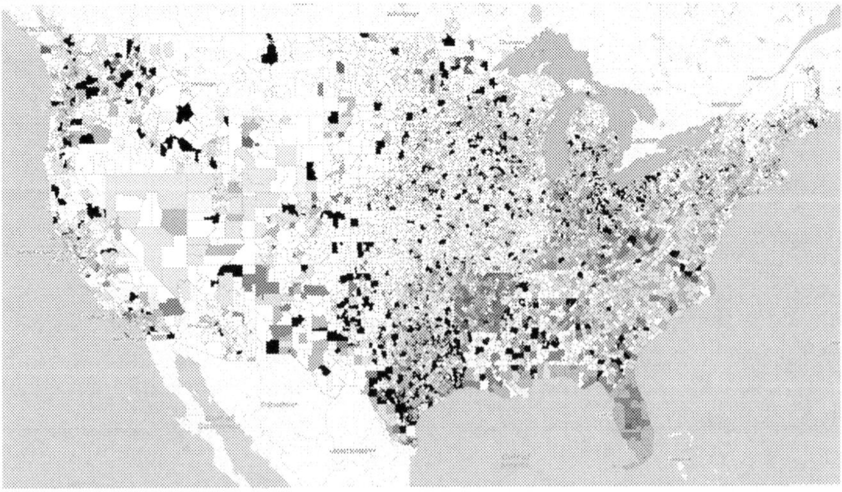

Note: Maps only illustrate unified school districts. Secondary-only districts are excluded from the illustration.

A larger and more detailed version of this map is available in the online appendix, available for free at https://www.tcpress.com/the-fractured-college-prep-pipeline-9780807765029

This study focuses on failure rates rather than passing rates for two reasons. Empirically, the CRDC only codes "no passing" if a student does not pass *any* of their AP exams. This means that if a student took two AP exams, they only get "no passing" if they failed to earn a 3 or higher (on an AP scale of 1 to 5) on both of the two exams. If they earned a 3 or higher on one or both of the exams, they would count as "passing" their exams. Theoretically, the impact of failing AP exams is more detrimental to college readiness than passing some or all of them.

Before explaining pass and failure rates, let's discuss the darkest areas on the map.

Not Proctoring Exams

As noted at the start of the chapter, 21st-century educational tracking breaks new ground in unequal outcomes by posing a novel challenge for students attempting to get college credit: One-quarter of AP students never experience an opportunity to take an exam in efforts to earn college credit. Districts on the map in Figure 6.1 that are shaded distinctly black are the CP districts where no students took any AP exam. These districts are scattered throughout the United States. Nationally, 12% of districts and 14% of charter schools do not proctor AP exams even though they teach AP to their students. Most of these districts (73%) are single-HS districts.

Figure 6.2 tallies the percentage of CP districts that simply flush their students out of the college-prep pipeline because they do not proctor an AP test to any of their students.[5] One in 3 Texas and Nebraska CP districts do not proctor AP exams, nor do around 1 in 4 CP districts in Kansas, Mississippi, and Ohio. This paragraph could continue to list the staggering numbers of the districts per state that follow this practice, but this is an instance where the graph really speaks for itself.

This pipeline flush is a common practice. So much so that only three states—Hawaii, Maryland, and Nevada plus the District of Columbia—do not participate in this practice (and Hawaii and DC are single districts). In Connecticut, Delaware, Florida, West Virginia, and Wyoming, only one district does not proctor any AP exams. Other than these few exceptions, shunting students from this opportunity to demonstrate their AP mastery is not unusual.

Further, Figure 6.3 compares the counts of the charter schools that do not proctor AP exams with those that do test among the 727 charter schools that offer AP. This practice occurs much more frequently in Arizona, California, Florida, Texas, and Wisconsin charter schools. More than half (56%) of Wisconsin's 34 charter schools fail to proctor an AP exam to their students taking AP courses.

Figure 6.2. Percent of AP Districts Not Proctoring AP Exams, by State

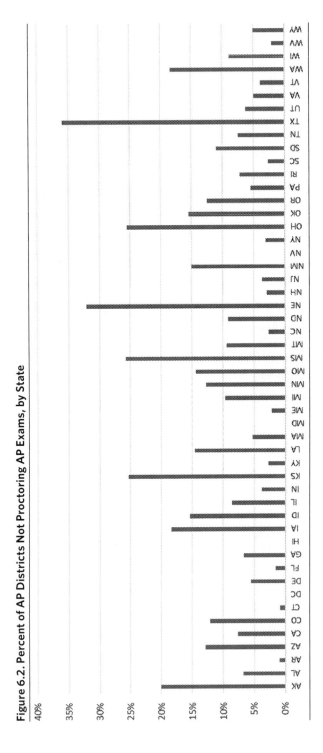

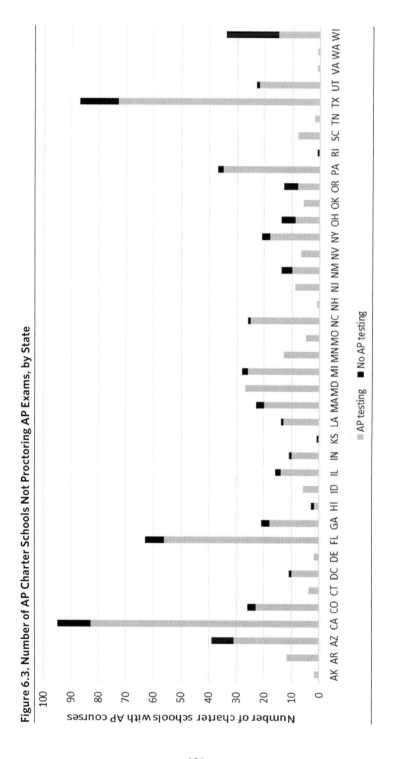

Figure 6.3. Number of AP Charter Schools Not Proctoring AP Exams, by State

Number of charter schools with AP courses

AP testing   No AP testing

AK AR AZ CA CO CT DC DE FL GA HI ID IL IN KS LA MA MD MI MN MO NC NH NJ NM NV NY OH OK OR PA RI SC TN TX UT VA WA WI

Stark differences in testing outcomes among the states exist, as these charts illustrate. The foundation of this chapter asks: How do district resources explain why some districts opt not to test any of their students taking AP courses? One set of models estimates the propensity for districts not to proctor an AP exam to any of their students whether they are a multi-HS district (Table A6.1, see online Appendix) or a single-HS district (Table A6.2, see online Appendix). These two models account for the state differences using a state fixed-effects model specification to test how resources impact the proctoring of an AP exam independent of legislative subsidies for exams.

Single-HS districts that receive Title I funds are 31% more likely to not proctor exams than their Title I multi-HS district counterparts. Other than this one major difference, there is virtually no difference between the multi-HS or single-HS district model estimates, even though so many of the districts that do not proctor AP exams are single-HS districts. These results mean that these resource factors may be more common among single-HS districts, but they do not "act differently" if the district has just one, several, or many high schools.

This ends up being mostly a story about size and 8th-grade test scores. Figure 6.4 shows how the chance of a district not proctoring an AP exam

Figure 6.4. Probability of Districts Not Proctoring Any AP Exam by 8th-Grade Standardized Scores

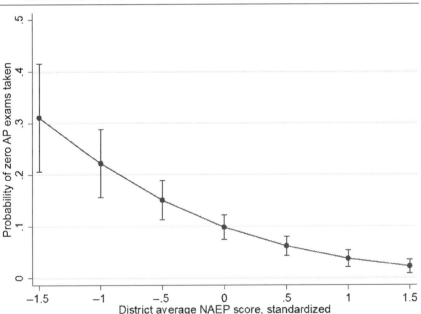

Predicted probabilities shown

Figure 6.5. Probability of Districts Not Proctoring Any AP Exam by Size of High School Population

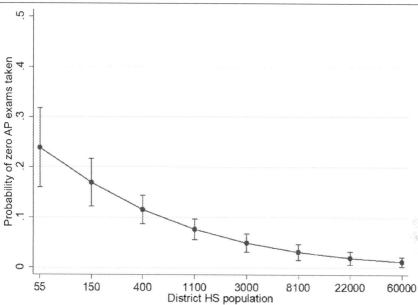

Predicted probabilities shown

relates to 8th-grade test scores: Districts that average about one standard deviation lower scores compared to the nation are twice as likely to not proctor AP exams as districts with average scores (see online Appendix Figure A6.1, Table A6.3 for each state). Figure 6.5 shows that size follows a similar logic: Smaller districts are less likely to proctor AP exams than larger districts. A small district with 400 high school students, for example, is twice as likely to not proctor AP exams as a medium district with 2,800 high school students.

For the charter schools, Table A6.4 in the online appendix shows that 8th-grade test scores work nearly identically among charter and public schools. Size does not matter for charter schools, but the student body composition does.

Unlike traditional public high schools, charter high schools serving higher proportions of Black, non-Hispanic students are less likely to not test; that is, they are more likely to proctor AP exams if Black, non-Hispanics make up a greater proportion of the student body. (But don't get too excited: The failure rates are much higher, as the subsequent pages of this chapter will show.)

Disparate impact on students. Which students are affected by whether or not there is a proctored exam? Figure 6.6 shows the differences in representation of students who take AP exams and those who attend schools that do

Figure 6.6. Student Representation Among Proctored AP Exams, by School Type

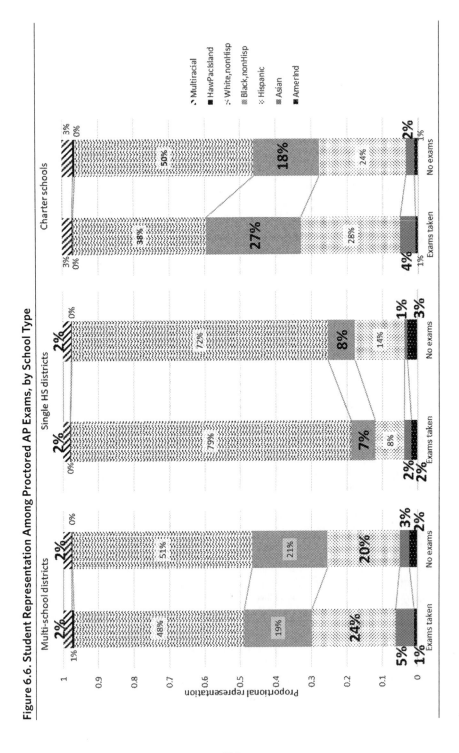

not proctor them. The small-font numbers on the chart show differences that may be large, but the models show that the individual racial or ethnic group differences are not distinguishably different than the rest of the student composition. Differences in representation that are shown in the big, bold font numbers on the chart show where students' racial or ethnic affiliation does significantly stand out as different than the rest of the student body composition. Across the board, there are no stark differences among White, non-Hispanic and Native Hawaiian or Other Pacific Islander students who are proctored the exam or not. In all settings, Asian students are overrepresented in schools that proctor exams. American Indian and Alaska Native and multiracial students are underrepresented in proctored exams in multi-HS and single-HS districts. Black, non-Hispanic students are underrepresented in proctored exam settings in single-HS districts but overrepresented in charter school settings. Hispanic students are overrepresented in multi-HS districts.

We return to the implications of not proctoring exams in the next chapter. Before that, let's explain why some groups of students do not pass any exams that they take.

Failing the AP exams: Who Fails and Why? This study is not interested in understanding why any individual student failed to earn a 3 or higher on their AP exam (which is the standard minimum score on the 1–5 scale to earn college credit as "passing" their high school AP course [Evans, 2019; Kolluri, 2018]). This study is interested, instead, in how it can be that groups of students fail to pass with a 3 or higher at some schools but not at others. Unlike valid arguments about the cultural bias in standardized tests, the AP exams directly base questions on the course material and thus are less subject to this testing bias.[6]

How many students fail all of their AP exams? Figure 6.7 shows the distribution for districts, and Figure 6.8 shows it for charter schools. In both, more than 16% of CP districts and 14% of CP charter schools have no students failing to earn a 3 or higher on their AP exams. On the other end, about 2% of districts and 2% of charter schools have all of their students failing all of their AP exams. In between these ends, the distribution is pretty flat for traditional public districts. For charter schools, the distribution is also quite evenly distributed, with a modest skew toward higher failure rates than lower rates.

When there are flat distributions like this, we must reconsider statistical specifications because these measures do not "act" like a normally distributed bell-curve continuous measure. In order to test hypotheses about how resources impact the prevalence of students failing to pass their AP exams, the outcome needs recoding so that the models can test the hypotheses with the most accuracy. For example, it might make sense to think that the district resources associated with 0% students failing exams are not the same as the resources associated with 100% of students failing all of their exams.

Figure 6.7. Proportions of AP Students in Districts Who Fail to Pass Any AP Exam

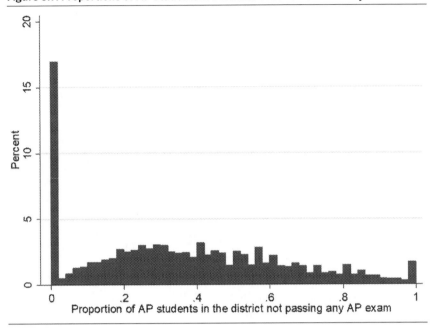

Figure 6.8. Proportions of AP Students in Charter Schools Who Fail to Pass Any AP Exam

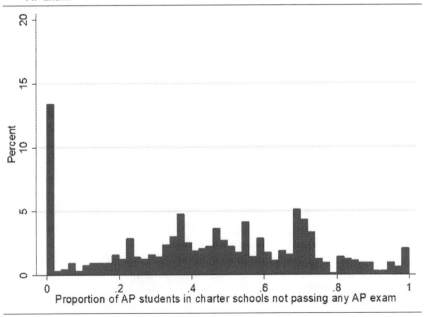

For this analysis then, the outcome recodes into groups of thirds plus the 0% and 100% markers. Thus, the models can compare how resources relate to districts with 0% (Zero), 1–33% (Low), 34–66% (Moderate), 67–99% (High), or 100% (All) of AP students failing to pass all of their AP exams. Table A6.5 in the online Appendix models the multinomial fixed-effects output explained in the following paragraphs.

First of all, the models show that failing rates of districts do not depend on the locale nor whether or not the district is a single-HS or multi-HS design. It also does not matter whether or not the district operates a CP-specialty school. However, districts with specialty schools find themselves with some failure; they are less likely to attain a Zero failure rate.

Other resources work differently, depending on whether we try to understand what relates to higher or lower rates of failure. Title I funding resources matter for the outskirt groups: Title I districts are 1.2 times more likely to have Zero failure (i.e., all students pass at least one of their exams) than districts without Title I. On the other end, however, Title I districts are 1.4 times more likely to be in the High failure rate group than districts without Title I funding. More extremely, districts receiving Title I funds are more than three times as likely to land in the All failure group than districts with otherwise equivalent resources that do not receive districtwide Title I funding.

Quite similarly to Title I, districts with small teacher rosters of less than 30 secondary-certified teachers are 1.5 times more likely to end up with Zero failure and yet 3.5 times more likely to end up in the All failure group compared to districts with moderate rosters of 30–100 teachers. Districts with large rosters of more than 100 secondary teachers are more likely to end up in the Low failure group and less likely to end up in the High failure group than equivalent districts with moderately sized teacher rosters.

Eighth-grade test scores also correlate with the failure rates. Figure 6.9 shows that districts with average 8th-grade achievement (mean of 0) are most likely to end up in the Moderate failure group with their AP students and least likely to end up with High proportions of exam takers failing. Districts with above-average 8th-grade scores are much more likely to have Zero of their students fail all their AP exams as well as these districts having less than a 1 in 5 chance of failing Moderate, High, or All of their AP students. Districts with below-average 8th-grade scores have the highest chance (2 in 5) that Low proportions of their AP students fail all their AP exams but about an equal chance that their students will coalesce to end up in the Zero, Moderate, or High failure groupings. The chance of districts ending up with 100% of AP students failing to pass all of their AP exams relates to 8th-grade scores.

Other than a few resources, the charter school models do not show resource differences associate much with their failure rates. The models shown in Table A6.6 (see online Appendix) show that charter schools specializing in CP are much less likely to have Zero students fail while being 3.6 times

Figure 6.9. Probability of District Failure Rates by 8th-Grade Achievement Scores

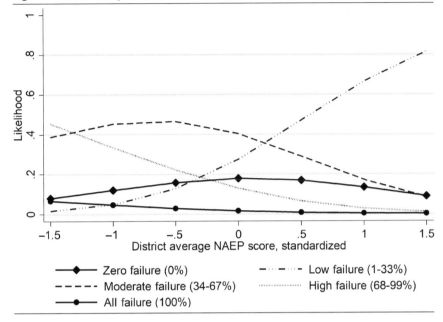

more likely to range in the Low failure grouping than other non-specialty CP charter schools. Small teacher rosters improve the chance of having Zero of their students fail all of their AP exams. Eighth-grade test scores work about the same in charter schools as in traditional districts.

All models for traditional public districts and charter schools show a troubling pattern: Student body composition relates directly to failure rates. Districts and charter schools with higher proportions of Hispanic and/or Black, non-Hispanic students are more likely to end up in the groups with high rates of students earning only a 1 or 2 on their AP exams. In charter schools, high failure rates overwhelmingly pervade if the schools enroll Hispanic or Black, non-Hispanic students.

Does school segregation explain these racial and ethnic composition factors? Hyper-segregation does not mitigate the racial/ethnic composition factor; failure rates increase *in addition to* the racial and ethnic composition in hyper-homogeneous districts. For charter schools, hyper-homogeneity does not affect rates since even the smallest enrollments of Hispanic and/or Black, non-Hispanic students outflank everything else in the model.

Together, these results mean that hyper-homogeneous districts serving students of color compound the chances that students will end up in schools where high rates of AP exam failure are commonplace. Moreover, charter schools serving Hispanic or Black, non-Hispanic students virtually guarantee high failure rates.

Not Passing: Racialized Outcomes

Remember the statement pages back about holding excitement about charter schools proctoring more exams? Figure 6.10 shows the percent of students who did not take any exam (even though they participated in AP), failed to pass any of their exams, passed an AP exam, and had "unknown results."

The unknown results show where data reported that these students participated in AP yet there is no information about their exam results. Upon a quick glance at the graph in Figure 6.10, it is obvious that the students affiliating with the smallest racial or ethnic heritages—American Indian or Alaska Native, Native Hawaiian or Other Pacific Islander, multiracial, and, to a lesser extent, Asian—have the largest unknown results gaps. Most of these "unknowns" are due to a practice in education research where we mask the results if the number of students is less than 10 in a subgroup. This is done by most states in order to protect students' privacy (NCES, 2010). Imagine, for instance, if there was only one Pan-Asian family attending a high school and then school results reported on their achievement scores— there would be no privacy for this family, and they could be at risk for retaliation from others in the school. Since these data are reported at the school level, there are lots of instances where the number of students taking, passing, or failing an AP exam is less than 10. When all these instances are added up, the graph shows how large chunks of students get "lost" in the data. A consequence of this legitimate reporting precaution is that we cannot assess whether or not these students are systematically served adequately or disenfranchised in their schooling experience.

The unknown results are larger in charter schools because charter schools generally enroll fewer students per school. This means that there is a greater chance that their subgroupings of students will fall below the 10 threshold.[7]

Comparing within groups, Figure 6.10 shows that the failure rates of Hispanic and Black, non-Hispanic students in charter schools are 1.5 times greater than their peers in traditional schools. It is important here to remind readers that far more students attend traditional public schools: 21 times more Hispanic students and 13 times more Black, non-Hispanic students sit in CP course seats in traditional schools compared to charter schools.

Figure 6.10 shows that charter schools fail to proctor exams to White, non-Hispanic, Native Hawaiian or Other Pacific Islander, and multiracial students at higher rates than traditional schools. Traditional schools fail to proctor exams to American Indian or Alaska Native, Hispanic, and Black, non-Hispanic students at higher rates than charter schools.

It appears that the difference in how students fail to earn a passing score—by either never taking the exam versus failing to pass it—ends up producing nearly identical pass rates. In the end, only about 1 in 3 Hispanic students (30% in traditional, 35% in charter) and 1 in 6 Black, non-Hispanic

Figure 6.10. AP Exam Results by Students' Race and Ethnicity

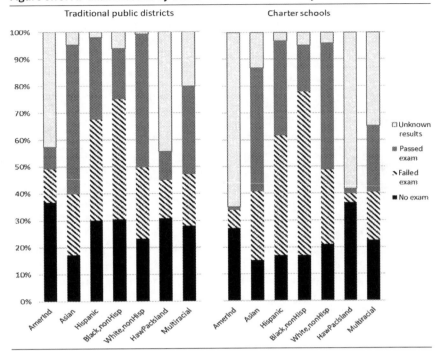

students (19% in traditional, 17% in charter) pass an AP exam. Whether they attend a traditional or charter school hardly impacts their efforts to earn the coveted 3 or higher AP exam score; pass rates are low in either school setting.

For all other students identifying as American Indian or Alaska Native, Asian, Native Hawaiian or Other Pacific Islander, multiracial, or White, non-Hispanic, a greater proportion pass their exams if they take AP courses at traditional schools than if they attend charter schools.

Together, a general conclusion is that charter schools do not help students pass AP exams. Charter schools associate with lower passing rates for most students. At best, charter schools offer no substantial difference in passing rates for Hispanic and Black, non-Hispanic students.

SUMMARY: STAGE 3 OF THE PIPELINE

This chapter reaches the end of the college-prep pipeline. The hypotheses tested how resource differences link to whether or not students earn that 3 or higher on their AP exam that they can then exchange for college course

Figure 6.11. Resource Hypotheses Explaining Variation in Stage 3

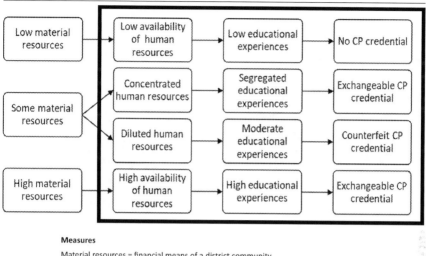

Measures

Material resources = financial means of a district community

Human resources = teachers qualified and available to teach college prep

CP credential = value of high school college prep curriculum for college

credit (see Figure 6.11). This analysis showed how a lack of resources creates structures where some schools cannot provide enough quality in their curriculum and then students fail to pass their exam. Other schools are so underresourced that no exam is even proctored for students to show their level of mastery over the subject matter.

Resources related to locale matters little at this point in the pipeline. Resources related to the availability of teachers to teach high-quality courses matter. Resources related to Title I funding matter, albeit in a complicated manner: For exam success, it hurts larger districts and helps smaller ones. But to succeed at exams, they need to be proctored, and Title I single-HS districts are much less likely to even proctor the exam to gauge success.

The level of achievement that follows students from their middle school years impacts the quality of coursework students receive as well.

Most students attending charter schools inordinately receive poorer-quality AP learning than their peers in traditional schools. Hispanic and Black, non-Hispanic students, however, receive grossly poorer-quality AP coursework no matter where they attend high school.

Before moving on to the next chapter that explains the whole puzzle now that all the pieces are put together in these analytic chapters, attention turns to discuss how the end of this pipeline works for the spotlight states.

Figure 6.12. Spotlight States: AP Exam Results by Students' Race and Ethnicity

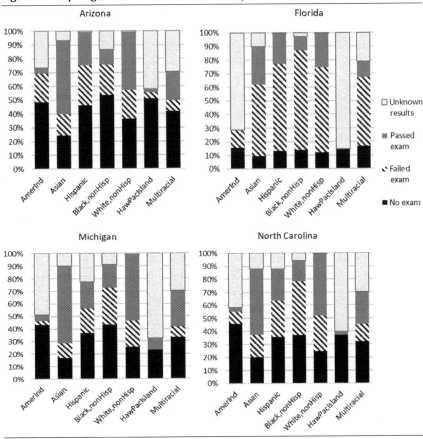

SPOTLIGHT STATES: HOW DOES AP TESTING
WORK WITHIN STATES?

When we look at the testing success across the spotlight states, we see some variation from the U.S. average discussed above. The impact of the "unknown results" shown in Figure 6.12 depends on the demographics of the state. In states like Arizona with larger student populations with heritages indigenous to the United States, there are fewer unknowns about this subgroup of students, while in Florida the success of this subgroup of students is far less known.

In Arizona, although more American Indian or Alaska Native and Hispanic students take exams, their failure rate is higher than their other Arizona peers in AP. There is little disparity in fail rates between Black, non-Hispanic and White, non-Hispanic students in Arizona. The same is not true in any other spotlight state.

In Michigan, more students pass than do not pass their AP exams, except for Black, non-Hispanic students. In Michigan, though, about 10% (34 districts) of their CP districts do not proctor any AP exams. This compares to the districtwide no testing only occurring in eight Arizona districts, four North Carolina districts, and one single Florida district.

Contrasted to North Carolina where the pass-fail ratios vary most disparately, three American Indian or Alaska Native and Black, non-Hispanic students fail for each one who passes, one Hispanic student fails for every one passing, nearly twice as many multiracial and White, non-Hispanic pass for each who fails, and nearly three Asian students pass for each who does not. The pass-fail ratios are nearly the same in Arizona as well, with only less disparity among Black, non-Hispanic students but slightly more among Hispanic students.

When we look at the four spotlight states, the wide variety of state regulations around high school education becomes apparent. Arizona has high rates of students who do not take any AP exam in their CP school. Comparatively, Florida seldom does not test. The proportion of students with no proctored exam in Michigan, and somewhat in North Carolina, looks close to the national norms of 25–30%. It is here that state policies really matter. The Florida legislature subsidizes AP exams and provides benefits to schools based on the proportion of students who earn a 3 or higher score (Education Commission, 2020). Michigan and North Carolina pay for college exams (e.g., ACT, SAT) plus heavily subsidize AP testing for students qualifying as low income (Education Commission, 2020). Arizona does not use state dollars to pay for any college exams (Education Commission, 2020). It seems that funding issues may explain why some schools do not test any of their students.

As discussed in the prior section, proctoring exams is important to allow students an opportunity to show their level of mastery. But, as we learned from the charter/traditional comparison at the national level, proctoring the exam does not relate to higher pass rates. In all four states, fewer Asian and White, non-Hispanic students experience "no exam" than their peers in their states.

In Florida, where we see high rates of AP exams proctored, we also see much higher failure rates than the national averages. The failure rates far outweigh the pass rates no matter how the data are disaggregated by racial or ethnic identity. In this 2013–14 database, zero American Indian or Alaska Native Floridian students passed among the 88 who took the AP exam. Further, only 1 in 8 Black, non-Hispanic Floridian students pass their proctored exams. Twice as many Hispanic, multiracial, and White, non-Hispanic Floridian students pass compared to their Black, non-Hispanic peers.

Figure 6.13. Correlation of Failure Rate to High School District Enrollment

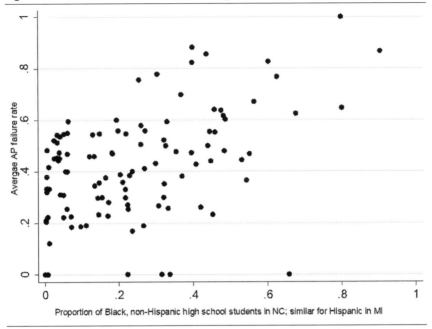

Proportion of Black, non-Hispanic high school students in NC; similar for Hispanic in MI

Michigan and North Carolina test results per student subgroup look similar to the national averages despite their large differences in district structure and size. When the models run separately on each of these four states (see Table A6.7 online), the pass rates of Black, non-Hispanic students in North Carolina and those of Hispanic students in Michigan are significantly worse than average. The graph in Figure 6.13 for the North Carolina data represents the correlation of Black, non-Hispanic student district populations and failure rates. It is important to remember that this graph shows the broad district high school representation and is not just about the students in the AP classrooms. While the graphic shows the North Carolina data, the Hispanic district population in Michigan follows a similar pattern.

The point about individual state standards also surfaces when we look at these spotlight states. Within each state model, the size of the district does not relate to the rate of not passing the AP exam. Rather, districts with large teacher rosters in Florida and North Carolina have higher failure rates. In Florida, single-HS districts also have higher failure rates. Resources tied to Title I districts is what matters in North Carolina districts. Comparatively, these teacher and monetary resources do not impact the failure rates in Arizona or Michigan.

As with the national models, locale is not a resource that factors into the equation at this point in the final stage of the pipeline.

CONCLUSION

We have now reached the end of the college-prep pipeline where less than 1 in 12 American students earn a college-prep credential that they can exchange for college credit. The analysis showed that 1 in 4 students in AP courses never even have the chance to show their mastery because their district never proctored an exam to them. Among the remaining 3 in 4 students in AP courses who did take at least one AP exam, about 1 in 3 fail it (score of 1 or 2).

The map showed a strong clustering in the data separating districts by state. Some states like Alabama, Arkansas, Florida, Hawaii, Kentucky, Mississippi, and the District of Columbia serve poor-quality AP curriculum to the majority (more than 50%) of their students with high rates of 1's and 2's on the AP exams. When districts serve primarily students of color, outcomes related to poor quality surface: These districts' pass rates are low. Charter schools proctor exams more often to their students, but their pass rates are abysmal.

With respect to resources, higher failure rates are more common in districts with few secondary-teacher human resources available. Lower failure rates correlate to districts with larger rosters of secondary-teacher human resources available. Title I funding does not impact multi-HS districts' exam results. However, when Title I supplements community resources in single-HS districts, it increases the chance that these districts will not proctor exams. Simultaneously, the pipeline analysis shows that when single-HS districts do proctor the exams, the Title I district pass rates are higher than their non-Title I counterparts.

The idea that 8th-grade scores impact whether or not districts even test their students is ethically abhorrent. If AP is delivered to students, schools are responsible for ensuring that high quality accompanies it in the classroom. To reiterate a point made earlier in the book, at no point is individual blame assigned for a nationwide social problem. However, these data help work toward equity in educational opportunities by identifying systematic inequality that creates fractures in the college-prep pipeline, reducing the quality of curriculum students receive. If students sit in AP classrooms, they should receive a sufficiently high-quality instruction that they can have a chance to demonstrate their mastery on an exam in hopes to earn their credential exchangeable for college credit (Sadler et al., 2010).

Exam preparation could be a learning opportunity in and of itself for students that they miss when they are not provided the chance to take the exam. If the reason for not proctoring an exam is the lack of getting through the material, then the onus is on the education organizations to develop pedagogical strategies to help teachers access resources for student success (Sadler et al., 2010). Sidelining students is not an acceptable strategy.

COMING UP NEXT

The start of the book explained that we needed to assemble chunks of the puzzle before putting it all together. The assembly showed fractures in the pipeline: from systemwide flushes of students out of it to junctures where students leaked out among their stream of classmates who stayed in the pipeline. Among the three stages of access, participation, and mastery, the puzzle shows the centrality of resources in shaping these opportunities to learn.

The next chapter does not focus on the resources that factor into these disparities. Instead, it puts together all the pieces to focus on the kids. It looks exclusively at how this complicated, multistage, multi-shunting pipeline impacts students and their educational opportunities. It considers how this impacts their high school learning and how it follows them into college.

CHAPTER 7

College-Prep Credentials
Who Gets Nothing, Who Gets Swindled, and Who Gets the Real Quality

The prior chapters assembled the sections of the pipeline puzzle. Each section described how resources shaped the opportunities for students to learn and prepare for college coursework. We talked about the interlocked stages of the pipeline that determine these high school opportunities. At each stage, resources define why some students get the opportunities to learn this advanced material and others do not. This chapter focuses on the endgame of this pipeline puzzle: How future college educational successes of U.S. high school youth are defined by these opportunities and their ability to engage in them.

The pipeline begins to shunt students out almost immediately (see Figure 7.1). In theory, all high school students should be eligible at the start of this precollege pipeline, but not all districts or charter schools teach college-prep curriculum, or they limit their prep to certain schools. For more than 1 in 9 students in U.S. high schools, the first step of the pipeline is the exit as they simply cannot access this curriculum. If a student is American Indian or Alaska Native or White, non-Hispanic in a rural area, this is often where the pipeline ends; the same holds true for urban Black, non-Hispanic students.

In Stage 2 of the pipeline, the students lucky enough to make it through the first stage by simply being in a school that offers college-prep curriculum, then actually have to sit in the prep classrooms. The absence of these classes on student schedules creates the second shunt, the largest of the entire pipeline. Black, non-Hispanic student representation plummets, and there are virtually no signs of students indigenous to the United States, Hawaii, or the Pacific Islands at this point in the pipeline. Yes, they see their peers in these classrooms, but only from the hallway view.

In the final stage, students can be shunted through two separate mechanisms: They fail to get the opportunity to take the AP exam, or they fail to pass the exam due to the poor quality of their college-prep courses. American Indian or Alaska Native and Black, non-Hispanic students tend to be flushed out via the lack of testing: They inordinately attend schools that do not proctor exams. Hispanic and Black, non-Hispanic students leak out

Figure 7.1. College-Prep Pipeline: Opportunity by Student Totals Across Racial and Ethnic Identity

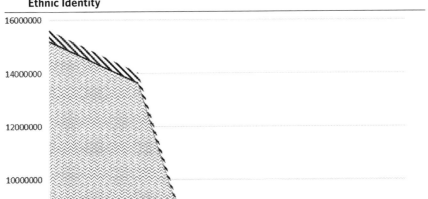

due to higher failure rates much more than their peers. Moreover, thousands of American Indian or Alaska Native, Native Hawaiian or Other Pacific Islander, and students identifying with two or more racial groups stand in the shadows in the pipeline of "unknown" since there is no data on their final credential.

By the end of this fractured pipeline, only 7–8%[1] of American high school students in 2013–14 gained a college-prep credential that they can exchange for college credit. When this dataset is qualified, the picture gets worse: This number only includes students in "regular" high school, so the number becomes even smaller if we consider the thousands of students who attend high school while in juvenile detention, hospital settings, or other state-run facilities.

Figure 7.2 frames the representation and equality issue from another angle. If the pipeline treated students equally and there was no disparity, the graph would show parity and look exactly the same from the left to the right with no changes in the proportions. That is, the proportions of students in the total high school population would flow through and look the same through to the end of the pipeline. Think of Figure 7.2 as representing a graduating high school class, with those who make it to the end successfully wearing sashes that declare they've passed their exams. In this mental image, those wearing sashes look much more White, non-Hispanic and Pan-Asian during graduation compared to the rest of the senior class.

Figure 7.2. College-Prep Pipeline: Opportunity by Student Representation Across Racial and Ethnic Identity

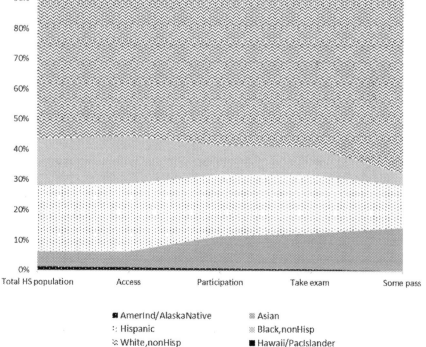

SEGREGATED LEARNING

Pieced together, a picture of segregated learning opportunities persists in the 21st century. Opportunities to learn college-prep curricula clearly pattern racial, ethnic, and residential (locale) disparities, allowing segregation to extend its reach into the college classroom. Some students can prep for college, and others cannot in a system defined by unequal resources in cases like *Milliken v. Bradley* (1974) and undergirded by residential segregation. To answer one of the original questions: The national push for "college for all" and "college ready" clearly do not mean the same thing across the United States, and they differ depending on the high school that students attend.

Impact of Resources

How do districts and charter schools sustain educational attainment gaps that disenfranchise entire groups of students while advantaging other groups? Resources. The short answer is about the haves and the have-nots of resources: which teachers work where, how school buildings get used, and what money gets allocated and spent. Coleman described this as a "diseconomy of resources" (1990), where students who attend districts rich in material and human resources gain more chances for opportunities while students who attend districts with more limited resources experience disenfranchisement from these opportunities (see also Domina et al., 2017). These resource findings stand even after accounting for state differences and ability theories on prior achievement. These findings reverberate through decades of unequal schooling in the United States (Domina et al., 2017).

We know from others' work that material resources correlate with the racial composition and poverty levels of schools (Horvat & O'Connor, 2006; Konstantopolous, 2006; Phillips & Chin, 2004). Emerging research documents the intersection of geographic isolation with resources (Curran & Kitchin, 2019). The COVID-19 pandemic also called attention to this resource gap by geography. Other research describes how the sociological organization of schools—the school environment, students' assignment to school, and curricular resources—shapes students' learning and educational outcomes (Hallinan, 1987, 1988). Together, if the organization of schools is defined by resources and resources are tied to student composition by way of historical segregation, we then can understand how segregated learning still pervades 21st-century American schooling among the students with the highest college expectations set upon them.

This pipeline analysis goes beyond the single-stage within-school tracking research, but many of the conclusions from that line of research appear to apply to the other stages in this longer pipeline. Similar to the three variations in magnet schools' curricular differentiation practices described by Metz in 1986, schools and districts also seem to split into different types of practices. School organizations appear to sort their material and human resources in such ways as to provide either low, moderate, high, or segregated college-prep opportunities to their students. These resource practices ultimately lead to a graduating class of high school seniors with drastically unequal college-prep experiences.

The supplemental analyses of charter schools test the refrain that districts act as structural constraints on schools to aptly use resources. The preceding chapters clearly demonstrate that the district-to-school organizational structure is not an additional constraint and that segregated learning opportunities operate in both the traditional and charter settings. It seems that charter schools may offer more opportunities at the onset of the pipeline, but their successful production of a quality college-prep credential to exchange for college credit ultimately trails behind the quality found in traditional public schools.

The inclusion of the 8th-grade achievement data in these analyses tests the refrain that prospective abilities shape how educational organizations design the learning platforms for their high school students.[2] At most stages in the pipeline, it is the case that the average tested ability of the district does directly impact opportunities for the high school students: whether their districts decide to dedicate a whole school to college prep rather than to all students in all schools, whether schools decide to proctor an exam, or the likelihood that many students will pass or fail the exams. Interestingly, though, the range (i.e., standard deviation) of tested 8th-grade achievement rarely relates to the pipeline structure. If the objective logic of this argument was to hold that the structure of opportunities would vary relative to prospective abilities, then we would expect to see that the variance of the 8th-grade test scores would matter, not the raw average score (Hallinan, 1992).

The findings on 8th-grade achievement creates an ethical question: If districts expend resources to enroll students in AP courses and then not one student took the exam or passed it, why were the resources spent this way? What resource failures occurred so that not one student succeeded? Where was the failure in the structure if the opportunity failed to meet the students' needs? Why did the structure facilitate the façade of college prep when it could only deliver a counterfeit credential?

Impact on Students

What are the consequences of those inequities for American high school students? At each stage, some students remain in the pipeline while others exit. These disparities compound over the pipeline's interlocked stages, and by the end of it at high school graduation, many students are left with far fewer college-ready skills than their peers. Some students may even earn false credentials, such as a marker of AP on their transcript but no AP exam score to exchange for college course credit. This false credential inserts a new social problem into 21st-century tracking not seen in earlier years: the rise of the "counterfeit credential" that has little exchange value in the college marketplace.

These findings show great variation in this educational transaction: Some students receive an exceptional experience that affords them college advantage, while others receive an inferior, or counterfeit, credential that has little to no exchange value. Other students never get the chance to earn the currency, while still others never even know there is a currency in existence.

The policy push for college readiness, combined with the rhetoric of "college for all" expectations, creates the demand for college-prep curriculum in high school (Rosenbaum, 2001; Schneider & Stevenson, 1999). Districts that serve 90% of American high school students heeded the demand for college-prep curriculum. Due to the optional nature of the AP and IB curriculum—that is, they are not part of states' standards—the quality of the delivery of the supply goes unregulated by any educational governing body.[3]

Figure 7.3 summarizes how groups of students fare in the college-prep marketplace. Much greater numbers of American Indian or Alaska Native students never interact with the college-prep currency compared to their peers. American Indian or Alaska Native and Black, non-Hispanic students also sit in far fewer seats in AP or IB classrooms and so never get the chance to earn the currency that they see their peers striving to earn. The students of color, with the exception of Asian students, who make it all the way through to the end of the pipeline often end up earning the counterfeit credential. This course title on their transcript may help on college applications, but it is the students who live in non-rural America and who identify as White, non-Hispanic and/or Asian who walk into college among their peers with the real currency to bypass introductory college courses, save tuition dollars, and possibly graduate earlier.

This book highlights the racial composition of schools and districts not because there exists some inherit relationship of skin complexion or ethnic heritage to learning—this would be absurd. It is highlighted to understand the sociological mechanisms of opportunities to learn that produce racialized divisions in the American schooling system. In the line of the classic opportunities-to-learn research, Hallinan clearly explains, sociologists need to better understand why social composition is a mechanism for opportunities to learn (1988). This investigation calls to action educational policymakers to address this social problem in the American schooling system as to why racial or ethnic heritage is a "sticky" factor despite the average rigor of learning rising across the United States, as shown by Doherty (2008), Kane (2004), Kao and Thompson (2003), Khalifa et al. (2016), Lucas (2009), and Mickelson (2003), among others.

Figure 7.3. College-Prep Pipeline: Credentialing Across Racial and Ethnic Identity

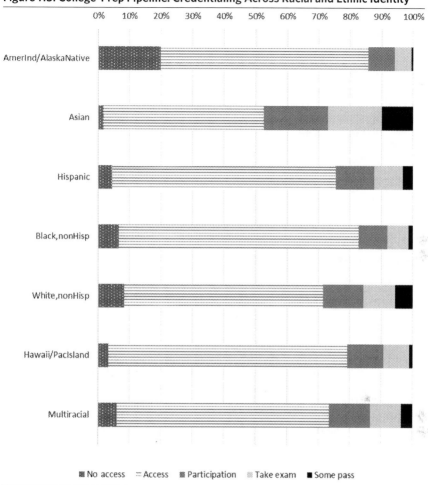

Note: The "unknown" test results are excluded from the totals in the figure.

Spotlight States: Segregated Learning

Before diving more deeply into the historical reverberations of this rise of counterfeit credentials, let's take a few pages to spotlight the four states to show how things vary among jurisdictions where the populations of students vacillate by history, geography, and current migration patterns.

As a reminder, if all else was equal, the shading in Figure 7.4 would look exactly the same from left to right on each state's graph. The changes in the graph show where chances for opportunities change from the prior stage in the pipeline.

Figure 7.4. Spotlight States: College-Prep Pipeline Opportunities by Student Representation Across Racial and Ethnic Identity

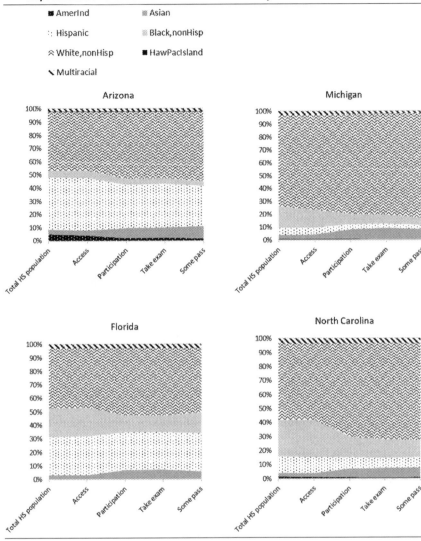

In Arizona, the change between the total high school population and attendance in a district with access starts to shunt American Indian or Alaska Native students right away. In Michigan, changes immediately occur at this first stage for Black, non-Hispanic students. Alternatively, Florida and North Carolina experience very little change, and their picture remains virtually the same early in the pipeline.

The change in middle stages from access to participation to taking the exam (i.e., who is left from those who were excluded due to no exam proctored) appears to impact Black, non-Hispanic students in all states except Arizona. Instead, Arizona continues to shunt its Native students and also shunts Hispanic students during these middle stages.

Across all the states, the picture for Asian students changes midstream at the participation stage in the CP pipeline. After that stage, the representation of Asian students remains relatively flat for the rest of each state's picture.

In Arizona, the shunting of American Indian or Alaska Native students from the picture occurs through to the end of the pipeline. Between the middle and the end, Hispanic students are also shunted from the picture. At the last stage of passing exams, Arizona's Black, non-Hispanic representation becomes shunted.

The almost exclusive shunt on Black, non-Hispanic students in Florida is stark. It is only at the last stage of the pipeline that the White, non-Hispanic students who made it through to the end get shunted. It is only in Florida where a group resurges after an earlier exit from the pipeline. At the final stage, it seems that the White, non-Hispanic students who sat in the CP classrooms—when the Black, non-Hispanic students were shunted prior—get outperformed by the Black, non-Hispanic students who took the exams.

In Michigan, American Indian or Alaska Native, Hispanic, and Black, non-Hispanic students are repeatedly shunted at every stage in the pipeline. Throughout these same stages, White, non-Hispanic students gradually gain opportunities.

North Carolina also shunts its American Indian or Alaska Native, Hispanic, and Black, non-Hispanic students in the pipeline's participation stage. Once students are enrolled in CP, the picture becomes quite flat and stable with the exception of Black, non-Hispanic students, who experience one last shunt at the end of the pipeline with passing exams.

Summary: Segregated Learning

We have now assembled all the pieces of this puzzle. Whether we look at the national picture or the individual states, the pictures unequivocally tell the same story: Students of color get shunted via flushes or leaks out of the pipeline disproportionately more than White, non-Hispanic students. Pan-Asian students seem to bypass most exits out of the pipeline, with the only difference at the participation stage. Whatever the verb—shunted, flushed, leaked, or exited—the conclusion is the same: Unequal opportunities abound in the current U.S. high school experience, and this inequality has a direct impact on the college experiences of the nation's students.

Why was it necessary to present the data in so many ways? Because ideas of equality in educational opportunities have many vantage points. These different presentations show how opportunity looks "from the inside" of who is sitting in the classroom and also "from the outside" of who is sitting around their family dinner tables talking about their school day. Depending on the state and location within the state, classrooms and family dinner tables look and feel different. All of the differences are what make the American puzzle complex, and it is also what makes it unlike any other place in the world. Together, these multiple vantage points allow us to see the American high school learning picture in all of its diversity.

When this century turned, so too did the way that segregated learning occurs. The introduction of No Child Left Behind (NCLB) in 2001 brought a new set of federal standards to schools, and its unintended consequences as well as its subsequent legislations created new structures in learning. The curricula differences of the 20th century are no longer found via de jure segregated schools, but they are instead de facto in rural schools as well as in suburban and urban tracked schools with no college-prep curriculum or CP-specialty schools with especially high concentrations of it.

Stopgaps and changes in 20th-century funding legislation set out to equalize opportunities. While Title I supplements do assist in some select contexts, they most often do not work to increase college-prep learning opportunities. The funding issues related to NCLB compliance testing cannot be understated because they have not been resolved, and the Great Recession compounded financial constraints. Together, school resources have been indefinitely cut since the turn of the century (Dee & Jacob, 2010; Leachman et al., 2017; Ravitch, 2016). Additionally, the rhetoric around NCLB disparaged teachers from entering and staying in the workforce and districts are making due with fewer highly qualified teachers in classrooms (Carver-Thomas & Darling-Hammond, 2017; Ford et al., 2017; Sutcher et al., 2016). These results show how the movement of teachers away from the school sector impacts the quality of curricula.

Opportunities to learn theory are based on the logic that student effort and ability are multiplied by the quality of the educational setting (Sørenson & Hallinan, 1977). The educational settings include not only the classroom, but also the school setting of teacher expertise, peer context, and academic climate (Gamoran et al., 1995; Sørenson & Hallinan, 1977). These results show how the most basic human and material resources define the breadth and depth of exposure to advanced course-taking in students' educational settings. It would only follow that as more resources could be associated with these outcomes, the size of the resource multiplier could only enlarge.[4] A 2019 study revealed that approximately 20% of schools enrolling mostly Black and Brown students receive upwards of one-third less funding than schools enrolling mostly White students (EdBuild, 2019). Without a stimulating educational setting, students' efforts and abilities cannot be realized (Sørenson, 1987). As the setting increases in quality, so too does the multiplier and thus the realization of students' efforts and abilities (Attewell & Domina, 2008; Kelly, 2007; Sørenson, 1987).

NEW TO THE EDUCATIONAL MARKETPLACE:
THE COUNTERFEIT CREDENTIAL

Tracking used in the 21st century now includes counterfeit credentials. "Counterfeit" engages the notion of a fake being passed off as real. Good counterfeits look and feel real to most people and may even pass as real to several people before they are recognized as a fake. The credential of "AP" and "IB" on a transcript will appear as real unless the exam results identify them otherwise.

Neo-Marxists might explain this phenomenon as a way to calm the masses with a façade of equality in order to avoid revolution of the majority of the have-nots. Rational choicers might explain the false credential as a new currency to distinguish the majority from the elite top. As mentioned in the beginning of the book, the intentionality aspect of this phenomenon is left to the theorists to develop and debate.

These educational capital ideas are not new. Collins described schooling as "cultural currency" (1979), and Bourdieu and Passeron (1977) explained two distinct types of educational capital: objectified and embodied. Bourdieu and Passeron (1977) explain how the exam acts as the standard to assess whether or not the student *embodied* the cultural capital necessary to succeed in the current educational system. Thus, when students gain their exam credential, they acquire an exchangeable educational currency that determines the level of opportunity for social mobility. The exam doubly serves to legitimate the curriculum because the external auditor appraised the quality of the teaching of the course material. Without the exam credential, a student can use the signal of the course title on their transcript to show acquisition of *objectified* cultural capital, but its exchange value is lessened since it can only show an accumulated educational good without any third-party appraisal of its value (Bourdieu & Passeron, 1977). This objectified cultural capital may help gain entrée into an educational sphere, such as admission to college, but the elite strata will require a signal of embodiment. As a result, the college-prep course itself as an objectified cultural good does have greater educational exchange value than no good at all, but its value is less than that of an embodied educational disposition.

Third-party exams work to maintain the social hierarchy using seclusion and exclusion, yet their external evaluation also provides a pinhole of opportunity to infiltrate the establishment by gaining admission to the elites' domain (Bourdieu, 1984).

Bourdieu's divergence into cultural capital stemmed from his thinking on the structural power of education. He explains in his works that the cultural undertones of the educational system maintain the status quo social structure because education cannot be disentangled from its political history (Bourdieu & Passeron, 1977).[5] The cultural embeddedness in the U.S.

educational structure continues to be tangled in its historical past of oppression and segregation (see also Khalifa et al., 2016).

Some might argue that the counterfeit credential can be rectified using college-placement exams when students' schools did not proctor exams. To this, imagine how the time lag between the 11th- or 12th-grade class and the schedule of the college-placement exam would compare in fairness to their peers who were tested their spring semester in high school at the pinnacle of their curricular learning. Moreover, students routinely score below their abilities on college-placement exams because the mere act of needing a placement exam threatens self-efficacy in the student, and this threat impacts marginalized students' scores even more than other students (Deil-Amen & Tevis, 2010; Holland, 2008). It is precisely these very students who would need these supplemental college-placement exams because they are more likely to attend schools that do not proctor exams than their peers, as these analyses showed. Also, the stigma of "needing an extra test" to qualify invokes racial and ethnic trauma[6] tied to generations of historical oppression.

RESEARCH IMPLICATIONS

The goal with this project was to bring to the public discourse an understanding of how the U.S. educational structure has evolved in recent decades because "change can only be pursued when it is seen" (Khalifa et al., 2016, p. 27). Educational researchers worked tirelessly in the second half of the 20th century to bring to the forefront of public discourse the consequences of racially segregated schooling and the racialized tracking that followed. Through decades of work, policymakers began to restructure school settings in attempts to alleviate this social wrong.[7] As the educational policies reframed toward equality, research at the start of the 21st century turned attention away from opportunity structures to instead concentrate on the attainment and achievement of individual children.

As policymakers worked to equalize opportunities from the oppressive structures in de facto 20th-century education, a new set of consequences arose in the educational pipeline. The pipeline is long and complex, so it is not surprising that these compounded inequalities went undetected on the whole. In some instances, such as with the inequalities experienced by Hispanic students, the sediment of consequences builds more slowly and thus is less detectable when anyone studies just one stage in the pipeline. In other cases, such as with the inequalities experienced by Native students, the numbers can often be too small and thinned out across too many schools to detect a structural problem stemming from policy in the "less than 5%" or "less than 10 students" subgroups.

This study returns to the original design of opportunities to learn: schools and districts. This organizational-level perspective is critical because it is the ground floor on which unequal opportunities to learn were built in the American education system (Graham, 2005; Anyon, 2005; Clotfelter, 2004; Domina et al., 2017; Lucas, 2009; Lucas & Berends, 2002; Mickelson, 2001, 2003, 2005; Tyack, 1974). These analyses highlight how students are distributed to predefined structural positions (see Domina et al., 2017; Sørenson, 1987) in CP-specialty or no-CP tracked schools. A focus on this ground floor is necessary because the individual and classroom levels depend on the organization to provide the base conditions in which students' ability and effort can grow. Without the stimulus of schools and their resources, students' abilities and efforts cannot be fully realized (Gamoran et al., 1995; Gamoran et al., 2000; Oakes, 1985; Sørenson & Hallinan, 1977). This ground floor of opportunities to learn, especially between schools, needs to be viewed as a source of inequality in American education and "the linchpin of social stratification" (Grodsky et al., 2008, p. 400).

Until the Office of Civil Rights established their projects to collect this census of curricular data, there was no national accounting of the structural differences that could be driving individual students' attainment and achievement gaps. Projects like this one bear the fruits from these data collection projects in hopes to again turn public discourse toward the systemic issues embedded in the American educational system that ultimately impact students' life outcomes through their disparate learning environments.

Researchers have been calling for some account of curricular quality and rigor across the decades (see Coleman, 1990; Gamoran, 1987; Gamoran et al., 1995; Blossfeld & Shavit, 2000; Minor, 2015; Minor et al., 2015). Datasets like this one only provide a crude measure of pass/fail, but the data are useful because they do not vary by state standards, regulations, or laws.

Much of the 20th-century tracking of children focused on the other end of the academic spectrum and how students were isolated into vocational schools or to the lower tracks of classes (Lucas & Berends, 2002). It seems that the 21st-century tracking of children now isolates children in the upper-middle end of the academic spectrum. A "moving up" average has been theorized before (Shavit & Blossfeld, 1993; Bourdieu & Passeron, 1977; Collins, 1979; Domina et al., 2017; Kerckhoff, 1993; Lucas, 1999; Perry et al., 2003; Rafterys & Hout, 1993). In essence, the pie might be getting larger, but the slices remain different sizes (Walters, 2000). This persistent inequality may not be a surprise to educational researchers, but it is likely a surprise to parents and students who thought that their college-prep classes signaled exclusivity and academic achievement. This study casts a spotlight on a flaw in the system that fails to check educational quality at the top end.

REFLECTION

This study emphasizes the impact on students from different racial or ethnic heritages because racialized schooling and differential learning opportunities are part and parcel of the history of American schooling (Anyon, 2005; Clotfelter, 2004; Graham, 2005; Orfield & Frankenberg, 2013; Reese, 2001; Tyson, 2011). This history recounts a clear, targeted, overt structure being instilled in the American schooling system to exclude Indigenous Peoples, people of color, and non-European immigrant students from equal learning opportunities from their White and European immigrant peers. Although U.S. laws evolved in the last 50 years, history embeds race into schooling that does not simply stop with new laws. Nor do simple school integration laws provide the linchpin solution (Lewis et al., 2015). The history runs deep in social norms, schooling expectations, and students' self-efficacy and educational stratification (Kerckhoff, 1993; Khalifa et al., 2016; Lewis & Diamond, 2015; Lucas & Berends, 2002; Tyson, 2011; Perry et al., 2003).

Social–psychological dispositions toward schooling shape the ways policymakers think about education, the needs of the students, and, as this book clearly showed throughout these analyses, how resources get allocated to meet those expectations and needs. While society may be hearing the siren call of college prep as the key to postsecondary success, resources have not followed to support all schools and districts in heeding this call.

In most states since the Great Recession, resources have stalled at pre-21st-century levels (American Federation of Teachers, 2018; Leachman et al., 2017). Educators appear to have turned to their toolbox to try to build a college-prep pipeline with strategies from 20th-century tracking to appeal to the siren call of college prep. It is not, then, a surprise that historical inequalities continue in this 21st-century tracking since the tools used were likely those from that age-old toolbox.

CONCLUSION

This educational pipeline is broken. Fractures abound at every stage. These fractures reproduce historical inequality. The counterfeit credential shrouds itself under the veil of a "college-prep" course title on a transcript. Without quality material and human resources, most students are left with an inferior learning experience that cannot be exchanged for college credit without extraordinary exceptions.

COMING UP NEXT

The final chapter in this book imagines the consequences in the near future if this educational disparity is not addressed. It provides some thoughts on how policymakers can act to address this new 21st-century educational inequality and act to equalize college readiness opportunities to learn. It ends discussing how this work on equality is only the tip of the iceberg to reach equity in learning.

CHAPTER 8

Implications and Thoughts on Moving Forward

This study thoroughly evidences that although more students experience college preparation than ever before, these opportunities to learn vary substantially. College ready outcomes in high school are structured differently across the United States and depend on where students attend. Some schools offer advanced college-prep courses, others do not. Some schools are effective at teaching these college-prep courses, others are not. What is common is that students do not have control over these meso-level structures, and yet their success is closely tied to the schools they attend (Gamoran et al., 2000; Mehan, 1992; Quillian, 2014).

This final chapter is written with the policymakers, college administrators, and students and their families in mind. It engages our imagination regarding the layers of de facto segregation that persist in educational opportunities in 21st-century America. For college students reading this book, consider the following questions: How did this inequality go unchecked for the past 20 years? How do politics and policies produce consequences of segregated opportunities to learn? For college admissions officers and administrators, what steps could colleges take to collaborate with districts in order to bridge the legitimacy gap between the college-prep enrollment and college course credit in efforts to improve college retention and graduation rates? For policymakers, how can policies and laws work toward equality of learning opportunity along all stages in the curricular pipeline without shunting students and repeating the policy consequences of the 20th century?

The four states used as case studies provide examples on which to build policies that work toward equality and learn from policies among varying political and historical contexts. The inclusion of the findings related to charter schools warn us not to assume that more choice in the educational system works to alleviate this problem.

HOW DID WE GET HERE?

Segregated learning opportunities by place and race are not new to the U.S. educational system. The *Milliken v. Bradley* (1977) ruling turned policymakers and politicians to center concerns on the within-district disparities in educational opportunities, which narrows the scope of the social inequalities in educational opportunities. As a result, the Office for Civil Rights investigations mainly focus on within-school disparities. This study demonstrates that the narrowed scope of investigations fails to show how some districts specifically house all their students in one single school. A within-schools analysis could show parity; however, the district-level analysis reveals segregation of college-prep resources between schools in the same district. Moreover, charter schools do not, ipso facto, provide relief from this problem.

While only the AP and IB curricula were analyzed in this study, the theoretical underpinnings of counterfeit credentials extrapolate to explain the unequal and continuing discriminatory outcomes in the U.S. educational system. The evidence in this book shows the cumulative divergence of opportunities to learn in the U.S. educational system for high school students. Other research demonstrates the divergence of opportunities during elementary school (Baumert et al., 2012; Lareau, 2000; Mickelson, 2001, 2015; Tach & Farkas, 2006), particularly around math in middle schools (Domina et al., 2016, 2019; Minor, 2015), and widely in postsecondary (Armstrong & Hamilton, 2013; Arum & Roksa, 2014; Attewell & Newman, 2010; Mettler, 2014). In addition, bias in disciplinary enforcement magnifies the loss in learning opportunities (Gregory et al., 2010, 2017; Latimore et al., 2018; Losen, 2011; Skiba et al., 2002, 2011; Steinberg & Lacoe, 2018).

The data and the theory presented in this book dovetail with educational studies on the resegregation of educational opportunities (Clotfelter, 2004; Frankenberg & Orfield, 2012; Mickelson, 2003; Orfield, 1996; Orfield & Lee, 2005, 2006; Quillian, 2014) as well as current research regarding the unequal learning experiences of students in American high schools (Frankenberg & Orfield, 2012; Gregory et al., 2010; Judson & Hobson, 2015; Mickelson, 2003; Rausch & Skiba, 2004; Skiba et al., 2011; Skiba et al., 2002). It complements studies on within-school segregation by moving the discussion forward to incorporate the between-school and between-district learning opportunity differences that are becoming the new approach to stratifying educational opportunities. It also shines a policy light on the growing educational racial disparities that were not addressed under (or were circumvented in response to) *Brown v. Board of Education*.

DATA ANALYSIS AND SOCIAL STRUCTURES

Social structures are not solid or tangible objects naked to the eye, but exist in history, culture, and norms understood through the collective experiences of people. With data like these, the existence of repeated, structured inequalities of learning opportunities can be quantitatively shown as indisputable social facts. The descriptions of why these patterns repeat and occur are debatable as a matter of theory and deeper data collection, but the social fact is real that students in some districts inordinately experience different learning opportunities than their peers in another zip code or from another ethnic or racial heritage.

One major advantage of using the Civil Rights Data Collection (CRDC) is that it is a census of all the AP and IB curricula across any publicly funded schools (i.e., traditional public and public charter schools), so there is no room for statistical error to make exceptions to the results. There is always the possibility that districts or schools "cook the books" and falsely report data to the federal government, but, as already mentioned, the threat of perjury and federal prosecution tends to dampen the likelihood of false reporting. The differences and descriptions here cannot be excused away as sampling bias or error.

However, regular, repeated data collections—even census ones like the biannually collected CRDC data used here—are threatened by Campbell's Law. Campbell recognized that *"the more any quantitative social indicator is used for social decision-making, the more subject it will be to corruption pressures and the more apt it will be to distort and corrupt the social processes it is intended to monitor"* (Campbell, 1979, p. 85, italics in original). In fact, the 2015–16 data that followed this 2013–14 dataset showed a drop in IB participation and a rise in dual enrollment courses, perhaps indicating a loophole in reporting procedures.

In 2015–16, there were many more schools that previously did not offer AP or IB that began to offer dual enrollment. While a separate study is needed to deconstruct all the details of this phenomenon of changing course offerings, suffice it to say that some of the districts that added dual enrollment as an option to their schools are the same ones that had some of the highest disparities in racial and ethnic representation in their AP classrooms. In a district just outside of Flint, Michigan, for example, the district that adopted new dual enrollment in one of their schools (that previously had no AP or IB) is the predominantly Black, non-Hispanic school among its other schools in the district. In 2013–14, the companion school that offers AP recorded extremely high segregation rates between student participation and exam success. But this does not tell the whole story. Ann Arbor Public Schools District also newly offered dual enrollment in 2015–16 in two of its high schools that previously had no AP or IB. In this case, the two schools are two of the smallest schools in the district. In these schools, the student populations mirror the other high school enrollments. In Ann Arbor, the segregation rates were near zero in 2013–14 when they then went on to adopt dual enrollment in these previously no-CP schools.

While a separate study is needed to deconstruct all the details of how dual enrollment is being implemented in districts, suffice it to say that sudden changes in district organization should warrant their own study. It is instructive for policy and organizational learning to understand where dual enrollment is becoming a collaborative bridge that overcomes resource gaps. It is important for civil rights to understand where it is being used under the guise of quality to veil another form of counterfeit college prep since dual enrollment numbers roll up whether students attend welding or college physics courses.

The CRDC monitoring does the social good of pointing districts to issues of disparity. It is then up to the districts to decide how to change the system of inequality, either by changing the internal workings of the district or handing off the issue to a third party. It could be the case that changes in course participation alerted district administrators to engage college instructors through dual enrollment to fill the human resource glut, or it could add panic to a district to do anything to look better "on the books" before the next audit.

Motivations cannot be determined with these current data. A qualitative study is needed for that question. At a minimum, a quantitative study needs data collected on dual enrollment course titles to tease apart which students get college prep versus which students receive career prep with dual enrollment. Both types of dual enrollment help educate students, but we need to monitor the equity in these opportunities for students.

Listening to district administrator voices about this issue is missing from this dialogue. We need to ask educators on the ground: What is the district doing to monitor the equality of learning opportunities? How can the name of a course indicate the expectations of rigorous learning? What policies ensure quality for all students? How does your district use audits like this one from the Office for Civil Rights to create internal decisions for students? If we are serious about resolving the inequalities in learning opportunities for students in the United States, then attention needs to be paid to Campbell's Law regarding the impact of monitoring on organizational decisions, behaviors, and policies.

While U.S. education policies are grounded in primacy of local context, U.S. history has shown that severe social ills of discrimination and prejudice thrive in unregulated spaces. Meyer and Rowan (1977) point to decoupling of school organizational design as a means to protect schools and education credentials from external scrutiny. This decoupling is said to be the foundation for unregulated legitimacy of schools. The federal collection of these data does not disrupt the lack of external scrutiny unless researchers invoke the data to assess quality across schools and jurisdictions.

COLLEGE ADMISSIONS

The national data already report rises in remedial coursework for entering students: from 35% in 2003–04 to 43% in 2015–16 (NCES, 2018). College professors seem surprised by this rise since rhetoric touts "college and career prep" as state mottos for high school education. The counterfeit credential may partly explain the disconnect between the quality of educational achievement that colleges think they are admitting compared to the actual skills students demonstrate when they participate in the college classroom.

Imagine the consequences if a critical number of colleges were to cease to exchange any high school college-prep work. How will admissions requirements change if course titles on transcripts fail to meet expectations? What happens if college admissions officers feel defrauded by the high school transcripts or college faculty push back on the legitimacy of students' incoming high school credentials? While democratization of college prep is intended to open and equalize opportunities for students, the public and legislative push to implement college prep with inferior resources can work to "put the cart before the horse." It may also pull resources from other school programs (Sadler et al., 2010). As this study showed, the consequence of this is a reduction of quality, rigor, and integrity of the learning experience.

Local partnerships of high schools with colleges offer a bridge to overcome this gap. Partnerships can vary from infrastructure resource sharing (like dual enrollment) to professional development for secondary and tertiary teachers to develop equal opportunities and experiences for students to collaborations between college and high school counselors. College counselors could bridge this divide (Allen et al., 2008), but there is caution about selection bias and discrimination with some other studies (McDonough, 1997).

More broadly, state and national consortiums that bring together college and high school instructors may offer much promise. Opening a dialogue with those in the classrooms may offer rich pathways to improve and assure quality. Schools of education seem ripe to facilitate these collaborations.

Should college prep be in every school? The answers from "college for all" research (Rosenbaum, 2001; Schneider & Stevenson, 1999) clearly show the unintended consequences for students who lose valuable high school learning under this design. What this book is pressing us to consider is how college may be using these courses as signals for college opportunities without consideration for the unequal opportunities for students to engage in college prep during their high school years (see also Holland, 2019).

POLICIES ON THE HORIZON

What can we learn from schools and districts that equitably deliver quality college-prep coursework to their high schoolers? Among our spotlight states, districts in college towns repeatedly surface as those organizations operating with the least disparity along all three stages in the pipeline *and* with signals of high quality. (Remember: Districts can have parity because no student gets to participate, so the quality again is important to hold in tow with opportunity.) Some of these districts, like Ann Arbor mentioned earlier, serve a diverse student population, while others are less diverse. In many of these college towns, funding is high and thus material resources are readily available. Moreover, human resources abound. Deeper understanding of the impact of funding, referenda, teacher workforce, and research–practice partnership collaborations would help us to understand why and how disparities are low while opportunities and experiences are high for so many students in these districts.

Although much of this study focused on racial and ethnic disparities, it is not the case that integrated schools are the "silver bullet" solution (see also Lewis et al., 2015; Tractenberg et al., 2020). As a reminder, the data clearly showed that the CP-specialty schools in multi-HS districts appeared the most diverse in enrollment, but often created the highest within-schools disparities in CP course participation. Parental information and inclusion in cross-neighborhood schools often lead to further alienation of students' opportunities to learn (Eaton, 2001; Horvat & O'Connor, 2006; Lewis et al., 2015; Wells & Crain, 1997).

In addition to the data considerations for dual enrollment, future policies would benefit from some additional data collection details. For one, there is a need for some new standard to bring the "unknown results" students out of the shadows in quantitative datasets like this one. The precaution for the individual student anonymity is serious and not to be dismissed. Offering some level of reporting needs to occur, however, so that students do not get lost in the data. An option, for instance, would be to "aggregate up" where these students could be reported in datasets at the county or state level where state departments of education pool the results across districts for external monitoring audits like this CRDC. For another, the CRDC data do not have "unique counts" of students in their files. This means that policymakers cannot decipher from these data whether one Hispanic student takes four AP courses or four Hispanic students each take one course. As mentioned earlier in this book, the logic presented in this study circumvents this conundrum using proportional representation measures, but another equality question can be answered with unique student counts data. And, of course, the inability to understand Hispanic ethnicity results in relation to racial results is a limitation of these data. If we want to be able to tease apart how bias enters into differences in opportunities to learn, the factor of complexion matters. Research clearly shows that "passing as White" creates disproportionate advantages for some students over their peers who do not "pass" (Bonilla-Silva, 2019; Ladson-Billings, 2020; Steers-McCrum, 2018). Data that collects ethnicity *and* race, rather than *or*, can answer this type of research and policy question. All of these suggestions engage considerations for student confidentiality protections.

Intersectionality is also important to consider. To start this equality dialogue, this study did not engage gender, language, special education, or immigration status with these analyses. Gender status is available in the CRDC dataset to analyze separately and with racial or ethnic identity. Language and special education statuses are only available as stand-alone metrics. There is no immigration measure. Moreover, the impact of discipline differences on opportunities to learn cannot be understated. As cited in prior pages, racial and ethnic disparities in discipline are profoundly wide. How discipline differentially impacts college-prep opportunities and experiences is yet to be understood.

Policy development would also benefit from a dataset that houses some school descriptions that identify key characteristics of the learning orientation in the schools. Granted, this would be optimistic, but it would be helpful to parents and policymakers. Right now, school names and a paragraph on a school website is all that most people get to find a sense of the school learning climate. Instead, if schools self-identified as "CP-specialty" or "dual options only," then parents would be enabled to inquire further. Right now, enrollment patterns show that most parents get information about the learning climate from informal network information from acquaintances, neighbors, and friends (Posey-Maddox, 2014; Renzulli & Roscigno, 2005). This informal information network reproduces racial and ethnic inequality, sustains misinformation, and perpetuates social hierarchies of inequality of who is "in the know" (Ellison & Aloe, 2019; Posey-Maddox, 2014).

STUDENTS AND FAMILIES

Let us close by imagining how this counterfeit credential phenomenon impacts students. How must students feel when, with all the pride of a new college student, they set foot on campus and only then realize that they are less prepared than others? How do families process why their children have to pay tuition for remedial classes when they thought that college prep was supposed to be a ticket to set their children off on the best foot on the college campus?

Many students and their families take the rhetoric of "college for all" at face value, trusting that their school system is upholding the social compact of college readiness. Installing the counterfeit credential extension to the pipeline does not meet the needs of students and their families nor quell the siren call for college prep. It simply provides a false reality. It gives students play money that they only realize is counterfeit once they travel to the college marketplace to cash it in.

School administrators can mend trust with families who feel betrayed by the broken social compact regarding the promises of "college for all." School counselors are likely central to this process (Holland, 2019; Witenko et al., 2017). It is in the schools and districts that school leaders can tailor policies to the school history, local political processes, and teacher subcultures (Allen et al., 2008; Metz, 1986) to alleviate unequal opportunities to learn (Domina et al., 2017; Mickelson, 2003).

These efforts are needed to thwart the threat of a growing disregard for the legitimacy of high school coursework. It is necessary to adjust quality before colleges cease to exchange course titles as legitimate signals of academic rigor. No action further threatens the social compact regarding the college promise of social uplift.

CONCLUSION

This study shows that the stages along the high school college-prep pipeline introduce a series of interlocked structural barriers to students. These barriers do not serve a simple, objective gatekeeping function to maintain the integrity of the advanced, rigorous quality of college-prep curricula but instead reinforce segregated structures that unfairly distribute the public good of education to some students and not to others. The structure of this college-prep pipeline in American high schools constitutes a new form of tracking in the 21st century that has the real effect of monopolies over opportunities to learn for some students while shunting opportunities to learn for others. Even more, this new tracking introduces a façade of ubiquitous college readiness that veils the unequal learning opportunities that set students out into the college world with pockets full of counterfeit educational capital. These counterfeit credentials reinforce the historically oppressive system in U.S. education. Whether intentional or not, this new form of stratified learning is embedded in schools across the United States with lifetime consequences for individual students that collectively work to magnify racial, ethnic, and inequality in the United States.

If we are serious about using the institution of education to fully develop the potential of all children in an effort to reach the common good, it is imperative that we (1) truthfully look at the consequences of the institutional structure, (2) work to improve it so that it benefits every student, no matter their birthright or zip code, (3) continue to evaluate the structure as changes are implemented, and (4) reconcile injustices when our institutional structures inflict harm, indignity, and inequality among any of us.

Notes

Chapter 1

1. One recent and notable exception is the rise of the #OptOut movements in some large cities (see Mitra et al., 2016; Strauss, 2016).

2. Thanks to the anonymous reviewer who suggested this clear distinction for referencing curricular data.

3. This is not without controversy, as some vigorously contest using racially imposed terms to describe the culturally diverse group of Indigenous Peoples across the North American continent (Yellow Bird, 1999; Steers-McCrum, 2018). Since this study engages the identity of students in classrooms in U.S. educational organizations, the argument regarding the Native shared identity was the primary orientation for identity.

4. National Assessment of Educational Progress (NAEP) test scores are the only national assessment of differences in state-curriculum quality, but that is aggregated to the subject matter and not specific to courses in schools across districts.

Chapter 2

1. The 2015 data is the most recent data available at the time of this research.

2. See An and Taylor (2019) and Klopfenstein and Lively (2012) for further discussion.

3. See also the special issue in *Economics of Education Review* (Toma & Zimmer, 2012).

4. Title I funding for districts is based on community census data, not the actual student population (U.S. Census Bureau, 2017, https://www.census.gov/data/datasets/2017/demo/saipe/2017-school-districts.html.

5. Counts of counties: https://thefactfile.org/us-states-counties/; number of school districts per state (Glander, 2015); poverty by district (ACS data): http://proximityone.com/sddmi.htm

Chapter 3

1. These ranges reflect the middle 90% of the distribution (the 10th to 90th percentile scores) to give a sense of the range without the outliers inflating the range.

2. There is a working assumption that the 8th-grade students attend the feeder high school. While this may not be true for all students, it is not likely a biased assumption that some districts will have more or less feeder students than the next district. For districts that are not comprehensive K–12 districts, the state average is imputed for the secondary district since the feeder patterns of the elementary/middle districts were not readily available for this study.

Chapter 4

1. District Title I status identifies districts where at least 40% of the student body resides in low-income households (U.S. Department of Education, 2015).

2. There are no 8th-grade achievement data for Colorado in the SEDA for the relevant years of 2009–10 and 2010–11 that capture the achievement levels of the students in the 2013–14 high school college-prep courses.

3. As a robustness check, additional models used state fixed-effects specifications. The results are robust to this specification. The logistic specification is preferred because, theoretically, access to AP and IB, as stated in Chapter 1, is independent of state education policies and standards. Practically, fixed effects drop out Hawaii, Washington, D.C., and Maryland entirely due to the n-1 specification needed in fixed effects, and these states have nearly universal access among their districts. Thus, these hundreds of districts are dropped from a fixed-effects specification, and we can learn from these districts, and thus the nationwide logistic regression is the optimal specification.

4. Colorado did not have achievement data for the years in question, and so the models do run without any contribution of any Colorado district. Other models used Colorado, and the results are not substantially nor significantly different.

5. Where academic abilities are defined by performance on standardized tests. There is much debate around the operationalization of academic abilities using standardized test achievement scores. For further reading on this debate, see Au (2016).

6. It is particularly curious that charter schools with distance learning modes of delivery do not widely offer AP or IB since the human resource challenge should not present a barrier.

7. "Impoverished" district is defined simply as a district where all of the high schools in the district receive Title I funds.

8. Z-test of mean differences between districts with or without access within-state, p<.05. Colorado is excluded from these tests since they have no achievement data in the SEDA.

9. *Note:* These SEDA achievement data only capture the status of academic abilities of students, and this only partially predicts academic potential of students.

Chapter 5

1. With the notable exception of magnet schools, which seemed to be the exception to the critique since magnet schools were seen as an integration strategy to reduce white flight out of public schools in the late 20th century (Orfield, 1996).

2. Although locale is assigned at the district level (and thus is constant across all schools in the district), the percentages here compare the student enrollment numbers (individual level) who attend these schools rather than the counts of districts (organizational level). There are 9,083 schools in the 1,918 multi-HS districts (accounting for 26% of CP districts), plus 5,485 schools in single-HS districts (74% of CP districts).

3. SEDA data house school achievement scores for schools that serve grades 3–8, not high schools. These no-CP schools only occur in multi-HS districts. Feeder patterns between middle and high schools would be necessary to apply specific 8th-grade middle school scores to each of the high schools in these districts.

4. Two-level random effects logistic regression, controlling for state and District of Columbia using dummy variables. State cannot be a third-level in the model since

Hawaii and DC only have one district, and thus a third-level by state overidentifies the model.

5. Seventy percent of the 1,918 multi-HS districts universally hold Title 1 statuses across all of their high schools.

6. There are very few AP or IB schools where 100% of the students are taking AP or IB since high school students in grades 9 and 10 rarely have the prerequisites necessary to register for AP or IB courses. Specialty schools, for the purposes of this study, are coded when grade 9–12 high schools have an average minimum of 30% of its students in AP or IB courses. This empirically driven coding rests on the logic that nearly all students in grade 12 would be taking AP or IB, 20% of grade 11 students would qualify to take at least one college prep course, and grades 9 and 10 students would have 0% registration and would instead focus their coursework on taking the necessary prerequisite classes. The 30% threshold is adjusted accordingly for high schools that serve other grade configurations of grades 11–12 only, grades 10–12, grades 8–12, grades 7–12, and so forth.

7. In 2013–14 data, 101 schools were IB-specialty schools and 11% of these schools were charter schools.

8. In supplementary analyses (not shown here), the conclusions are similar if the analyses are limited only to compare multi-HS districts with a specialty school.

9. Supplemental analyses show similar patterns when looking at all districts, but the White, non-Hispanic student population is nearly twice as large and overwhelms the differences among students with other racial or ethnic heritages.

10. See also a thick description in the Shopping Mall High School (Powell et al., 1985). See also Kelly (2007) and Kelly & Price (2011).

11. Fixed-effects linear regression models, fixed for state plus Washington, D.C.

12. The one exception is the size of the district. In the full model, district size negatively correlates with proportion of CP coursework. A supplemental analysis used a quadratic variable to test if this flip was due to a u-shape threshold effect, but that was not the case. The number of secondary teachers accounts for the initial positive association with district size. Once teacher numbers are accounted for, the true correlation of district size shows as negative.

13. Seven-percentage-point change in the average proportion of CP coursework.

14. All Florida high schools are required to offer AP, IB, or dual enrollment courses (Education Commission, 2020). Dual is excluded from this analysis.

Chapter 6

1. When the IB testing data becomes accessible, these same ideas will be tested in a subsequent paper.

2. I am indebted to the research team at Stanford's Educational Opportunity Project for their foresight to develop this project and labor to produce these comparable data. For more information on this project, see https://edopportunity.org. The United States does have the National Assessment of Educational Progress, but this is not a mandated test of students and operates under a complicated set of regulations with light legal weight if schools refuse to participate (Institute of Education Statistics, 2020). The new Stanford Educational Data Archives uses statistical techniques to translate state testing data into comparable data across state lines for grades 3–8. This study uses this new dataset to test the ability theory argument.

3. NAEP test scores are the only national assessment of differences in state-curriculum quality, but that is aggregated to the subject matter and not specific to courses in schools across districts.

4. For this study, notwithstanding the subject matter specifics.

5. It could be the case that districts falsify their AP exam data to the federal Office of Civil Rights and falsely report that no student took an AP exam when, for instance, all students instead failed it. While this saving face could be taking place to save the embarrassment that no students passed, the misreporting of data to the federal government falls under perjury of law; thus it seems reasonable to work under the assumption that these data are true and free of this error since district administrators gain more risk by perjuring themselves with false numbers rather than reporting high failure rates.

6. There are relevant and valid arguments to make about the cultural bias embedded in the curriculum materials for AP and any other American subjects taught in high school. This concern does not induce systematic error into our models since it is a constant. However, the discussion is important to consider when discussing equity broadly. For great discussions, see Grodsky et al. (2008) and Holland (2008).

7. For a review of the consequences of thresholds like these as an administrative strategy to avoid federal sanctions, see Booher-Jennings (2005).

Chapter 7

1. This is not an exact number due to the "unknown" missing data. We know that 6.5% passed some AP exams, plus another 1.1% took IB courses. We also know that 93.2% did not pass any AP exam nor participate in IB, thus leaving a 1.1% discrepancy from "unknown results" on AP exams.

2. It says nothing about how learning disparities accumulated from K–8th grade (Mickelson, 2003).

3. The Office of Civil Rights is a federal governing body that does audit the supply of these curricula, but it is unable to regulate the quality of the supply.

4. On top of this multiplier effect, we know from research that marginalized students from impoverished or racial or ethnic minority backgrounds are more sensitive to the quality of their school and teachers (Downey et al., 2004; Nye et al., 2004).

5. Although in Bourdieu's study of the French system, this history is based on land ownership and nobility rather than the racial segregationist history of the United States (Bourdieu & Passeron, 1977).

6. Gender as well, but this study does not discuss this demographic in these analyses since there are few schools with wide variation on the 50/50 gender composition in high schools.

7. This says nothing regarding reparations for the generations of lost educational opportunities. For that discussion, see Khalifa et al. (2016).

References

Allen, W. (2020). Preface: Race: American education's inescapable conundrum. In R. T. Teranishi, B. M. D. Nguyen, C. M. Alcantar, & E. R. Curammeng (Eds.), *Measuring race: Why disaggregating data matters for addressing educational inequality*. Teachers College Press.

Allen, W. R., Suh, S. A., Gonzalez, G., & Yang, J. (2008). Qui bono? Explaining—or defending—winners and losers in the competition for educational achievement. In T. Zuberi & E. Bonilla-Silva (Eds.), *White logic, White methods: Racism and methodology* (pp. 217–238). Rowan & Littlefield Publishers.

American Federation of Teachers. (2018). A Decade of Neglect: Public Education Funding in the Aftermath of the Great Recession. https://www.aft.org/sites/default/files/decade-of-neglect-2018.pdf

American Psychological Association. (2020). *Publication manual of the American Psychological Association: Seventh Edition*. American Psychological Association.

An, B. P. (2013a). The impact of dual enrollment on college degree attainment: Do low-SES students benefit? *Educational Evaluation and Policy Analysis, 35*(1), 57–75.

An, B. P. (2013b). The influence of dual enrollment on academic performance and college readiness: Differences by socioeconomic status. *Research in Higher Education, 54*(4), 407–432.

An, B. P., & Taylor, J. L. (2019). A review of empirical studies on dual enrollment: Assessing educational outcomes. In *Higher education: Handbook of theory and research: Volume 34* (pp. 99–151). Springer International Publishing. https://doi.org/10.1007/978-3-030-03457-3_3

Anyon, J. (2005). Radical possibilities: Public policy, urban education, and a new social movement. Routledge.

Apthorp, H. S. (2016). Where American Indian students go to school: Enrollment in seven central region states. REL 2016-113. Regional Educational Laboratory Central, Issue. U.S. Dept. of Education.

Armstrong, E. A., & Hamilton, L. T. (2013). *Paying for the party*. Harvard University Press.

Arum, R., & Roksa, J. (2014). Aspiring adults adrift: Tentative transitions of college graduates. University of Chicago Press.

Asante, G., Sekimoto, S., & Brown, C. (2016). Becoming "Black": Exploring the racialized experiences of African immigrants in the United States. *Howard Journal of Communications, 27*(4), 367–384.

Attewell, P. (2001). The winner-take-all high school: Organizational adaptations to educational stratification. *Sociology of Education, 74*(4), 267–295.

Attewell, P., & Domina, T. (2008). Raising the bar: Curricular intensity and academic performance. *Educational Evaluation and Policy Analysis, 30*(1), 51–71.

Attewell, P., & Newman, K. S. (2010). *Growing gaps: Educational inequality around the world*. Oxford University Press on Demand.

Au, W. (2016). Meritocracy 2.0: High-stakes, standardized testing as a racial project of neoliberal multiculturalism. *Educational Policy, 30*(1), 39–62.

Austin, M. (2020). Measuring high school curricular intensity over three decades. *Sociology of Education, 95*(1), 65–90.

Barnes, G., Crowe, E., & Schaefer, B. (2007). *The cost of teacher turnover in five school districts: A pilot study*, National Commission on Teaching and America's Future.

Barnes, W. B., & Slate, J. R. (2013). College-readiness is not one-size-fits-all. *Current Issues in Education, 16*(1), 1–13.

Barrett, J. (2016, December 18). Betsy DeVos & Michigan education. *Lansing State Journal*. https://www.glep.org/betsy-devos-and-education-reform-in-michigan/

Baumert, J., Nagy, G., & Lehmann, R. (2012). Cumulative advantages and the emergence of social and ethnic inequality: Matthew effects in reading and mathematics development within elementary schools? *Child Development, 83*(4), 1347–1367.

Bifulco, R., & Ladd, H. F. (2008). Charter schools in North Carolina. In M. Berends, M. G. Springer, & H. J. Walberg (Eds.), *Charter school outcomes* (pp. 195–220). Lawrence Erlbaum Associates.

Billingham, C. M., & Hunt, M. O. (2016). School racial composition and parental choice: New evidence on the preferences of white parents in the United States. *Sociology of Education, 89*(2), 99–117.

Blazar, D. (2018). Validating teacher effects on students' attitudes and behaviors: Evidence from random assignment of teachers to students. *Education Finance and Policy, 13*(3), 281–309.

Blossfeld, H.-P., & Shavit, Y. (2000). Persisting barriers: Changes in educational opportunities in thirteen countries. In R. Arum & I. R. Beattie (Eds.), *The Structure of Schooling: Readings in the Sociology of Education* (pp. 245–259). Mayfield Publishing Company.

Bonilla-Silva, E. (2019). Feeling race: Theorizing the racial economy of emotions. *American Sociological Review, 84*(1), 1–25.

Bonilla-Silva, E., & Zuberi, T. (2008). Toward a definition of White logic and White methods. In T. Zuberi & E. Bonilla-Silva (Eds.), *White logic, White methods: Racism and methodology* (pp. 3–30). Rowman & Littlefield Publishers.

Booher-Jennings, J. (2005). Below the bubble: "Educational triage" and the Texas accountability system. *American Educational Research Journal, 42*(2), 231–268.

Borman, G. D., & Dowling, N. M. (2008). Teacher attrition and retention: A meta-analytic and narrative review of the research. *Review of Educational Research, 78*(3), 367–409.

Bourdieu, P. (1984). Distinction: A social critique of the judgement of taste. Harvard University Press.

Bourdieu, P., & Passeron, J.-C. (1977). *Reproduction in education, culture and society*. Sage.

Brady, L. M., Strong, Z. H., & Fryberg, S. A. (2020). The mismeasure of Native American students: Using data disaggregation to promote identity safety.

In R. T. Teranishi, B. M. D. Nguyen, C. M. Alcantar, & E. R. Curammeng (Eds.), *Measuring race: Why disaggregating data matters for addressing educational inequality* (pp. 131–153). Teachers College Press.

Brashears, M. E., Genkin, M., & Suh, C. S. (2017). In the organization's shadow: How individual behavior is shaped by organizational leakage. *American Journal of Sociology, 123*(3), 787–849.

Brewer, B., & Schufletowski, D. (2017). *Referendum recollection and projection.* Wisconsin Association of School Business Officials Spring Conference, Wisconsin. https://www.wasbo.com/images/WASBO/Documents/6/Handouts/SC2017 _ReferendumRecollectionAndProjection.pdf

Brody, L. (2018, July 11). Brooklyn parents have mixed feelings on school admissions proposal. *The Wall Street Journal.* https://www.wsj.com/articles/brooklyn -parents-have-mixed-feelings-on-school-admissions-proposal-1531354760

Campbell, D. T. (1979). Assessing the impact of planned social change. *Evaluation and Program Planning, 2*(1), 67–90.

Cannata, M. A., & Penaloza, R. (2012). Who are charter school teachers? Comparing teacher characteristics, job choices, and job preferences. *Education Policy Analysis Archives, 20*(29), 1–25.

Carnevale, A. P., Jayasundera, T., & Gulish, A. (2016). America's divided recovery: College haves and have-nots. Georgetown University Center on Education and the Workforce.

Carver-Thomas, D., & Darling-Hammond, L. (2017). *Teacher turnover: Why it matters and what we can do about it.* Learning Policy Institute.

Center for Evaluation, Policy & Research. (2018). *School referenda in Indiana.* https://cepr.indiana.edu/disr.html

Chemerinsky, E. (2002). The segregation and resegregation of American public education: The court's role. *NCL Rev., 81,* 1597.

Chingos, M., & Blagg, K. (2017). *How has education funding changed over time?* Urban Institute. https://apps.urban.org/features/education-funding-trends/

Christenson, B., Rossi, R., & Daugherty, S. (1996). *What academic programs are offered most frequently in schools serving American Indian and Alaska Native students?* (IB-3-96). Issue Brief. U.S. Department of Education.

Cipollone, K., & Stich, A. E. (2017). Shadow capital: The democratization of college preparatory education. *Sociology of Education, 90*(4), 333–354.

Cisneros, J., Gomez, L. M., Corley, K. M., & Powers, J. M. (2014). The Advanced Placement opportunity gap in Arizona: Access, participation, and success. *AASA Journal of Scholarship and Practice, 11*(2), 20–28.

Clotfelter, C. (2004). After "Brown": The rise and retreat of school desegregation. Princeton University Press.

Coleman, J. S. (1990). *Equality and achievement in education.* Westview Press.

College Board. (2014, February). *The 10th annual AP report to the nation.* https:// apstudent.collegeboard.org/creditandplacement/search-credit-policies

College Board. (2018). *AP credit policy search.* College Board. https://apstudent .collegeboard.org/creditandplacement/search-credit-policies

College Board. (2020). *AP at a glance.* College Board. https://apcentral.collegeboard .org/about-ap/ap-a-glance

Collins, R. (1979). *The credential society: An historical sociology of education and stratification.* Academic Press.

Comparative International Education Society [CIES]. (2019). *Educators in revolt: Global lessons from the recent wave of U.S. teachers' strikes*. Comparative International Education Society, San Francisco.

Crain, A. (2018). Serving rural students. *NACE Journal*, May. https://www.naceweb.org/career-development/special-populations/serving-rural-students/

Cucchiara, M. B., & Horvat, E. M. (2009). Perils and promises: Middle-class parental involvement in urban schools. *American Educational Research Journal*, 46(4), 974–1004.

Curran, F. C., & Kitchin, J. (2019). Documenting geographic isolation of schools and examining the implications for education policy. *Educational Policy*, 0(0). https://doi.org/10.1177/0895904819864445

Dee, T. S., & Jacob, B. A. (2010). *The impact of No Child Left Behind on students, teachers, and schools*. Issue, Brookings Papers on Economic Activity.

Deil-Amen, R., & Tevis, T. L. (2010). Circumscribed agency: The relevance of standardized college entrance exams for low SES high school students. *The Review of Higher Education*, 33(2), 141–175.

DeVoe, J. F., & Darling-Churchill, K. E. (2008). Status and trends in the education of American Indians and Alaska Natives: 2008. NCES 2008-084.

Diette, T. M. (2012). The Whiter the better? Racial composition and access to school resources for Black students. *The Review of Black Political Economy*, 39(3), 321–334.

Dika, S. L., & Singh, K. (2002). Applications of social capital in educational literature: A critical synthesis. *Review of Educational Research*, 72(1), 31–60.

Domina, T., Hanselman, P., Hwang, N., & McEachin, A. (2016). Detracking and tracking up: Mathematics course placements in California middle schools, 2003–2013. *American Educational Research Journal*, 53(4), 1229–1266.

Domina, T., McEachin, A., Hanselman, P., Agarwal, P., Hwang, N., & Lewis, R. W. (2019). Beyond tracking and detracking: The dimensions of organizational differentiation in schools. *Sociology of Education*, 92(3), 293–322.

Domina, T., McEachin, A., Penner, A., & Penner, E. (2015). Aiming high and falling short: California's eighth-grade algebra-for-all effort. *Educational Evaluation and Policy Analysis*, 37(3), 275–295.

Domina, T., Penner, A., & Penner, E. (2017). Categorical inequality: Schools as sorting machines. *Annual Review of Sociology*, 43, 311–330.

Domina, T., & Saldana, J. (2012). Does raising the bar level the playing field? Mathematics curricular intensification and inequality in American high schools, 1982–2004. *American Educational Research Journal*, 49(4), 685–708.

Donaldson, K. (2017). The implementation of the International Baccalaureate Diploma Program: Equity, access, and effectively maintained inequality. University of Notre Dame.

Dougherty, K. (2008). The community college: The impact, the origin, and future of a contradictory institution. In J. H. Ballantine & J. Z. Spade (Eds.), *Schools and society: A sociological approach to education*, (3rd ed., pp. 399–408). Sage Publishers.

Downey, D. B., Von Hippel, P. T., & Broh, B. (2004). Are schools the great equalizer? Cognitive inequality during the summer months and the school year. *American Sociological Review*, 69(5), 613–635.

Durham Public Schools. (2020). *Registering for school*. https://www.dpsnc.net/site/Default.aspx?PageID=210

Dvorak, P. (2018, February 26). D.C. school lottery: An academic "Hunger Games" parents are desperate to win. *The Washington Post.*

Eaton, S. E. (2001). *The other Boston busing story: What's won and lost across the boundary line.* Yale University Press.

EdBuild. (2019, July). *Dismissed: America's most divisive school district borders.* https://edbuild.org/content/dismissed/edbuild-dismissed-full-report-2019.pdf

Education Commission of the States. (2018, April). *State summative assessments 2017–18: All data points.* http://ecs.force.com/mbdata/mbquest5E?rep=SUM1806

Education Commission of the States. (2020). *Advanced Placement policies: All state profiles.* http://ecs.force.com/mbdata/mbprofallrt?Rep=APA16

Ellison, S., & Aloe, A. M. (2019). Strategic thinkers and positioned choices: Parental decision making in urban school choice. *Educational Policy, 33*(7), 1135–1170. https://doi.org/10.1177/0895904818755470

Epple, D., Romano, R., & Zimmer, R. (2016). Charter schools: A survey of research on their characteristics and effectiveness. In *Handbook of the economics of education* (Vol. 5, pp. 139–208). Elsevier.

Evans, B. J. (2019). How college students use Advanced Placement credit. *American Educational Research Journal, 56*(3), 925–954.

The Fact File. (2018). *List of U.S. states and number of counties in each.* https://thefactfile.org/us-states-counties/

Fahle, E. M., & Reardon, S. F. (2017). How much do test scores vary among school districts? New estimates using population data, 2009–2015. *CEPA Working Paper No.17-02,* Stanford Center for Education Policy Analysis. http://cepa.stanford.edu/wp17-02

Fenning, P., & Rose, J. (2007). Overrepresentation of African American students in exclusionary discipline: The role of school policy. *Urban Education, 42*(6), 536–559.

Finkel, S. E. (1995). *Causal analysis with panel data.* Sage Publications.

Flaherty, J. (2018, May 8). The teachers won. *Phoenix New Times.* http://www.phoenixnewtimes.com/news/the-teachers-won-how-arizonas-strike-unfolded-10403354

Ford, T. G., Van Sickle, M. E., Clark, L. V., Fazio-Brunson, M., & Schween, D. C. (2017). Teacher self-efficacy, professional commitment, and high-stakes teacher evaluation policy in Louisiana. *Educational Policy, 31*(2), 202–248.

Fraga, L. R., & Perez, N. (2020). Latinos in the American racial hierarchy: The complexities of identity and group formation. In R. T. Teranishi, B. M. D. Nguyen, C. M. Alcantar, & E. R. Curammeng (Eds.), *Measuring race: Why disaggregating data matters for addressing educational inequality* (pp. 29–45). Teachers College Press.

Frankenberg, E., & Orfield, G. (2012). *The resegregation of suburban schools.* Harvard Educational Press.

Freidus, A. (2016). "A great school benefits us all": Advantaged parents and the gentrification of an urban public school. *Urban Education, 54*(8), 1121–1148.

Freire, P. (1970). *Pedagogy of the oppressed.* Bloomsbury Publishing USA.

Gagnon, D. J., & Mattingly, M. J. (2012, Summer). *Beginning teachers are more common in rural, high-poverty, and racially diverse schools.* Issue Brief No. 53. University of New Hampshire.

Gagnon, D. J., & Mattingly, M. J. (2016). Advanced Placement and rural schools: Access, success, and exploring alternatives. *Journal of Advanced Academics, 27*(4), 266–284.

Gamoran, A. (1987). The stratification of high school learning opportunities. *Sociology of Education, 60*(3), 135–155.

Gamoran, A. (2007). *Standards-based reform and the poverty gap: Lessons for No Child Left Behind.* Brookings Institution Press.

Gamoran, A., & An, B. P. (2016). Effects of school segregation and school resources in a changing policy context. *Educational Evaluation and Policy Analysis, 38*(1), 43–64.

Gamoran, A., Nystrand, M., Berends, M., & LePore, P. C. (1995). An organizational analysis of the effects of ability grouping. *American Educational Research Journal, 32*(4), 687–715.

Gamoran, A., Secada, W. G., & Marrett, C. B. (2000). The organizational context of teaching and learning: Changing theoretical perspectives. In M. T. Hallinan (Ed.), *Handbook of the sociology of education* (pp. 37–64). Springer Science and Business Media.

Gawade, N. G., & Meyer, R. H. (2016). Measuring teacher effectiveness using value-added models of high school achievement. *Teachers College Record, 118*(13).

Geiser, S., & Santelices, V. (2006). *The role of Advanced Placement and honors courses in college admissions.* Center for Studies in Higher Education, University of California, Berkeley.

Gibson, C. (2010). *American demographic history chartbook: 1790 to 2000.* http://demographicchartbook.com/index.php/chapter-4-race-and-hispanic-origin/

Glander, M. (2015, July). *Selected statistics from the public elementary and secondary education universe: School Year 2013–14: First Look* (NCES 2015-151).

Goldrick-Rab, S., & Mazzeo, C. (2005). Chapter 5: What No Child Left Behind means for college access. *Review of Research in Education, 29*(1), 107–129.

Goyette, K. A. (208). College for some to college for all: Social background, occupational expectations, and educational expectations over time. *Social Science Research, 37*(2), 461–484.

Graham, P. A. (2005). *Schooling America: How the public schools meet the nation's changing needs.* Oxford University Press.

Grand Rapids Public Schools. (2020). *Applications and enrollment.* Grand Rapids Public Schools. https://www.grps.org/apply-to-a-school

Gregory, A., Skiba, R. J., & Mediratta, K. (2017). Eliminating disparities in school discipline: A framework for intervention. *Review of Research in Education, 41*(1), 253–278.

Gregory, A., Skiba, R. J., & Noguera, P. A. (2010). The achievement gap and the discipline gap: Two sides of the same coin? *Educational Researcher, 39*(1), 59–68.

Griffin, K. A., & Mwangi, C. A. G. (2020). Similar, but not the same: Considering the intersections of race, ethnicity, and immigrant status in the lives of black students. In R. T. Teranishi, B. M. D. Nguyen, C. M. Alcantar, & E. R. Curammeng (Eds.), *Measuring race: Why disaggregating data matters for addressing educational inequality* (pp. 103–118). Teachers College Press.

Grodsky, E., & Riegle-Crumb, C. (2010). Those who choose and those who don't: Social background and college orientation. *The Annals of the American Academy of Political and Social Science, 627*(1), 14–35.

Grodsky, E., Warren, J. R., & Felts, E. (2008). Testing and social stratification in American education. *Annual Review of Sociology, 34,* 385–404.

Gutiérrez, K. D., & Jaramillo, N. E. (2006). Chapter 9: Looking for Educational Equity: The Consequences of Relying on "Brown." *Yearbook of the National Society for the Study of Education, 105*(2), 173–189.

Hafoka, I., Vaughn, K., Aina, I., & Alcantar, C. M. (2020). The "invisible" minority: Finding a sense of belonging after imperialism, colonialism, and (im)migration for Native Hawaiian and Pacific Islanders in the United States. In R. T. Teranishi, B. M. D. Nguyen, C. M. Alcantar, & E. R. Curammeng (Eds.), *Measuring race: Why disaggregating data matters for addressing educational inequality* (pp. 67–83). Teachers College Press.

Hallett, R. E., & Venegas, K. M. (2011). Is increased access enough? Advanced Placement courses, quality, and success in low-income urban schools. *Journal for the Education of the Gifted, 34*(3), 468–487.

Hallinan, M. T. (1987). The social organization of schools: An overview. In M. T. Hallinan (Ed.), *The Social organization of schools: New conceptualizations of the learning process*. Plenum Press.

Hallinan, M. T. (1988). Equality of educational opportunity. *Annual Review of Sociology, 14*(1), 249–268.

Hallinan, M. T. (1992). The organization of students for instruction in the middle school. *Sociology of Education, 65*(2), 114–127.

Hallinan, M. T., & Sørenson, A. B. (1983). The formation and stability of ability groups. *American Sociological Review, 48*(6), 838–851.

Hanover Research. (2010, October). Current trends in International Baccalaureate programs. http://www.ibsom.org/uploads/9/0/6/3/9063770/current_trends_in _international_baccalaureate_programs_-_membership.pdf

Henry, G. T., & Redding, C. (2020). The consequences of leaving school early: The effects of within-year and end-of-year teacher turnover. *Education Finance and Policy, 15*(2), 332–356.

Holland, M. M. (2019). Divergent paths to college: Race, class, and inequality in high schools. Rutgers University Press.

Holland, P. W. (2008). Causation and race. In T. Zuberi & E. Bonilla-Silva (Eds.), *White logic, White methods: Racism and methodology* (pp. 93–110). Rowman & Littlefield Publishers.

Horvat, E. M., & O'Connor, C. (2006). *Beyond acting White: Reframing the debate on Black student achievement*. Rowman & Littlefield Publishers.

Hunter, M. (2007). The persistent problem of colorism: Skin tone, status, and inequality. *Sociology Compass, 1*(1), 237–254.

Iatarola, P., Conger, D., & Long, M. C. (2017). Determinants of high schools' advanced course offerings. *Educational Evaluation and Policy Analysis, 33*(3), 340–359.

Ingersoll, R., Merrill, L., & Stuckey, D. (2014). Seven trends: The transformation of the teaching force. Updated April 2014. CPRE Report.# RR-80. Consortium for Policy Research in Education.

Institute of Education Statistics. (2020, April). *2019–2020 NAEP participation.* Institute of Education Statistics. https://nces.ed.gov/nationsreportcard/participating/

International Baccalaureate Organization. (2020). *IB educator certificates.* https:// apstudent.collegeboard.org/creditandplacement/search-credit-policies

Jacob, B., Dynarski, S., Frank, K., & Schneider, B. (2017). Are expectations alone enough? Estimating the effect of a mandatory college-prep curriculum in Michigan. *Educational Evaluation and Policy Analysis, 39*(2), 333–360.

James, A. (2008). Making sense of race and racial classification. In T. Zuberi & E. Bonilla-Silva (Eds.), *White logic, White methods: Racism and methodology* (pp. 31–46). Rowman & Littlefield Publishers.

Judson, E., & Hobson, A. (2015). Growth and achievement trends of Advanced Placement (AP) exams in American high schools. *American Secondary Education, 43*(2), 59–76.

Jussim, L., & Harber, K. D. (2005). Teacher expectations and self-fulfilling prophecies: Knowns and unknowns, resolved and unresolved controversies. *Personality & Social Psychology Review, 9*(2), 131–155.

Kane, T. (2004). College going and inequality. In K. Neckerman (Ed.), *Social Inequality* (pp. 319–345). Russell Sage.

Kao, G., & Thompson, J. S. (2003). Racial and ethnic stratification in educational achievement and attainment. *Annual Review of Sociology, 29*(1), 417–442.

Keesler, V., Wyse, A., Jones, N., & Schneider, B. (2008). Calculating the ability of within-school teacher supply to meet the demands of new requirements: The example of the Michigan Merit Curriculum. REL Technical Brief. REL 2008-No. 005. Regional Educational Laboratory Midwest.

Kelly, S. (2007). The contours of tracking in North Carolina. *The High School Journal, 90*(4), 15–31.

Kelly, S. (2009). The black-white gap in mathematics course taking. *Sociology of Education, 82*(1), 47–69.

Kelly, S., & Price, H. (2011). The correlates of tracking policy: Opportunity hoarding, status competition, or a technical-functional explanation? *American Educational Research Journal, 48*(3), 560–585.

Kelly, S. P. (2004). Do increased levels of parental involvement account for social class differences in track placement? *Social Science Research, 33*(4), 626–659.

Kerckhoff, A. C. (1993). *Diverging pathways: Social structure and career deflections*. Cambridge University Press.

Kerckhoff, A. C. (2000). Transition from school to work in comparative perspective. In M. T. Hallinan (Ed.), *Handbook of the sociology of education* (pp. 453–474). Springer.

Kerckhoff, A. C., & Glennie, E. (1999). The Matthew effect in American education. *Research in Sociology of Education and Socialization, 12*(1), 35–66.

Kewal Ramani, A., Zhang, J., Wang, X., Rathbun, A., Corcoran, L., Diliberti, M., & Zhang, J. (2018). *Student access to digital learning resources outside of the classroom. NCES 2017-098.* Issue, National Center for Education Statistics.

Khalfani, A. K., Zuberi, T., Bah, S., & Lehohla, P. J. (2008). Race and population statistics in South Africa. In T. Zuberi & E. Bonilla-Silva (Eds.), *White logic, White methods: Racism and methodology* (pp. 63–92). Rowman & Littlefield Publishers.

Khalifa, M. A., Douglas, T.-R. M., & Chambers, T. T. (2016). White gazes of Black Detroit: Milliken v. Bradley I, Postcolonial theory, and persistent inequalities. *Teachers College Record, 118*(3), 1–34.

Kilgore, S. B. (1991). The organizational context of tracking in schools. *American Sociological Review, 56*(2), 189–203.

Klopfenstein, K. (2004). The Advanced Placement expansion of the 1990s: How did traditionally underserved students fare? *Education Policy Analysis Archives, 12*, 1–68.

Klopfenstein, K., & Lively, K. (2012). Dual enrollment in the broader context of college-level high school programs. *New Directions for Higher Education*, 158, 59–68.

Klugman, J. (2012). How resource inequalities among high schools reproduce class advantages in college destinations. *Research in Higher Education*, 53(8), 803–830.

Kolluri, S. (2018). Advanced Placement: The dual challenge of equal access and effectiveness. *Review of Educational Research*, 88(5), 671–711.

Konstantopoulos, S. (2006). Trends of school effects on student achievement: Evidence from NLS: 72, HSB: 82, and NELS: 92. *Teachers College Record*, 108(12), 2550–2581.

Kozol, J. (1991). *Savage inequalities: Children in America's schools* (1st ed.). Crown Publishers.

Lacireno-Paquet, N., Holyoke, T. T., Moser, M., & Henig, J. R. (2002). Creaming versus cropping: Charter school enrollment practices in response to market incentives. *Educational Evaluation and Policy Analysis*, 24(2), 145–158.

Ladson-Billings, G. (2020). Who's Black? Hybridity, complexity, and fluidity in 21st-century racial identity. In R. T. Teranishi, B. M. D. Nguyen, C. M. Alcantar, & E. R. Curammeng (Eds.), *Measuring race: Why disaggregating data matters for addressing educational inequality* (pp. 15–28). Teachers College Press.

Lankford, H., Loeb, S., & Wyckoff, J. (2002). Teacher sorting and the plight of urban schools: A descriptive analysis. *Educational Evaluation and Policy Analysis*, 24(1), 37–62.

Lareau, A. (2000). *Home advantage: Social class and parental intervention in elementary education*. Rowman & Littlefield Publishers.

Lareau, A. (2015). Cultural knowledge and social inequality. *American Sociological Review*, 80(1), 1–27.

Lareau, A., & Calarco, J. M. (Eds.). (2012). *Class, cultural capital, and institutions: The case of families and schools*. Russell Sage Foundation.

Lareau, A., & Horvat, E. M. (1999). Moments of social inclusion and exclusion: Race, class, and cultural capital in family-school relationships. *Sociology of Education*, 72(1), 37–53.

Latimore, T. L., Peguero, A. A., Popp, A. M., Shekarkhar, Z., & Koo, D. J. (2018). School-based activities, misbehavior, discipline, and racial and ethnic disparities. *Education and Urban Society*, 50(5), 403–434.

Lauen, D. L. (2007). Contextual explanations of school choice. *Sociology of Education*, 80(3), 179–209.

Leachman, M., Masterson, K., & Figueroa, E. (2017). A punishing decade for school funding. *Center on Budget and Policy Priorities*.

Lee, J., & Lubienski, C. (2011). Is racial segregation changing in charter schools? *International Journal of Educational Reform*, 20(3), 192–209.

Lee, V. E., Smerdon, B. A., Alfeld-Liro, C., & Brown, S. L. (2000). Inside large and small high schools: Curriculum and social relations. *Educational Evaluation and Policy Analysis*, 22(2), 147–171.

LeTendre, G. K., Hofer, B. K., & Shimizu, H. (2003). What is tracking? Cultural expectations in the United States, Germany, and Japan. *American Educational Research Journal*, 40(1), 43–89.

Lewis, A. E. (2004). "What group?" Studying Whites and Whiteness in the era of "color-blindness." *Sociological Theory*, 22(4), 623–646.

Lewis, A. E., & Diamond, J. B. (2015). *Despite the best intentions: How racial inequality thrives in good schools*. Oxford University Press.

Lewis, A. E., Diamond, J. B., & Forman, T. A. (2015). Conundrums of integration: Desegregation in the context of racialized hierarchy. *Sociology of Race and Ethnicity, 1*(1), 22–36.

Lewis, A. E., & Embrick, D. G. (2016). Working at the intersection of race and public policy: The promise (and perils) of putting research to work for societal transformation. *Sociology of Race and Ethnicity, 2*(3), 253–262.

Lin, N. (2000). Inequality in social capital. *Contemporary Sociology, 29*(6), 785–795.

Losen, D. J. (2011, October 5). *Discipline policies, successful schools, and racial justice*. The Civil Rights Project, National Education Policy Center.

Loveless, T. (1999). Will tracking reform promote social equity? *Educational Leadership, 56*, 28–32.

Lucas, S. (2009). *Theorizing discrimination in an era of contested prejudice: Discrimination in the United States*. Temple University Press.

Lucas, S. R. (1999). *Tracking inequality: Stratification and mobility in American high schools*. Teachers College Press.

Lucas, S. R. (2001). Effectively maintained inequality: Education transitions, track mobility, and social background effects. *American Journal of Sociology, 106*(6), 1642–1690.

Lucas, S. R., & Berends, M. (2002). Sociodemographic diversity, correlated achievement, and de facto tracking. *Sociology of Education, 75*(4), 328–348.

Lumina Foundation. (2020). *Community Partnerships Cohort Map*. Lumina Foundation. https://www.luminafoundation.org/campaign/talent-hubs/community-partnerships/

Ma, J., Pender, M., & Welch, M. (2016). *Education pays 2016: The benefits of higher education for individuals and society*, College Board. https://files.eric.ed.gov/fulltext/ED572548.pdf

MacDonald, V. M. (2001). Hispanic, Latino, Chicano, or "Other"? Deconstructing the relationship between historians and Hispanic-American educational history. *History of Education Quarterly, 41*(3), 365–413.

Mackel, T. (2018, June 26). Jefferson Parish parents cry foul after charter school lottery do-over. *WDSU News*. http://www.wdsu.com/article/jefferson-parish-parents-cry-foul-after-charter-school-lottery-do-over/21952518

MacLeod, J. (1987). *Ain't no makin' it: Aspirations and attainment in a low-income neighborhood*. Routledge.

Malkus, N., Hoyer, K. M., & Sparks, D. (2015). Teaching vacancies and difficult-to-staff teaching positions in public schools. Stats in Brief. NCES 2015-065. National Center for Education Statistics.

Martin, J. L. (2009). *Social structures*. Princeton University Press.

Mathews, J., & Hill, I. (2006). *Supertest: How the International Baccalaureate can strengthen our schools*. Open Court.

Mathis, W. J. (2005). The cost of implementing the federal No Child Left Behind Act: Different assumptions, different answers. *Peabody Journal of Education, 80*(2), 90–119.

McDonough, P. M. (1997). *Choosing colleges: How social class and schools structure opportunity*. SUNY Press.

McFarland, J., Hussar, B., Wang, X., Zhang, J., Wang, K., Rathbun, A., Barmer, A., Cataldi, E. F., & Mann, F. B. (2018). *The condition of education 2018*. NCFE Statistics. https://nces.ed.gov/pubsearch/pubsinfo.asp?pubid=2018144

Mehan, H. (1992). Understanding inequality in schools: The contribution of interpretive studies. *Sociology of Education, 65*(1), 1–20.

Merisotis, J. (2017, September 14). *We need radical change to hit 60 percent by 2025*. Lumina Foundation. https://www.luminafoundation.org/news-and-views/we-need-radical-change-to-hit-60-percent-by-2025/

Mettler, S. (2014). *Degrees of inequality: How the politics of higher education sabotaged the American dream*. Basic Books.

Metz, M. H. (1986). *Different by design: The context and character of three magnet schools*. Routledge & Kegan Paul.

Meyer, J. W., & Rowan, B. (1977). Institutionalized organizations—Formal structure as myth and ceremony. *American Journal of Sociology, 83*(2), 340–363.

Michigan Department of Education. (2017). *Michigan Merit Curriculum: High school graduation requirements frequently asked questions*. https://www.michigan.gov/documents/mde/Complete_MMC_FAQ_August_2014_467323_7.pdf

Mickelson, R. A. (2001). Subverting Swann: First- and second-generation segregation in the Charlotte-Mecklenburg schools. *American Educational Research Journal, 38*(2), 215–252.

Mickelson, R. A. (2003). When are racial disparities in education the result of racial discrimination? A social science perspective. *Teachers College Record, 105*(6), 1052–1086.

Mickelson, R. A. (2005). How tracking undermines race equity in desegregated schools. In A. Stuart & J. Petrovich (Eds.), *Bringing equity back: Research for a new era in American educational policy* (Part II) (pp. 49–76). Teachers College Press.

Mickelson, R. A. (2015). The cumulative disadvantages of first- and second-generation segregation for middle school achievement. *American Educational Research Journal, 52*(4), 657–692.

Mickelson, R. A., & Everett, B. J. (2008). Neotracking in North Carolina: How high school courses of study reproduce race and class-based stratification. *Teachers College Record, 110*(3), 535–570.

Mid-America Research Institute. (2001, June). *Legislative History of .08 Per Se Laws* (DOT HS 809 286). Issue, National Highway Traffic Safety Administration. National Highway Traffic Safety Administration. https://one.nhtsa.gov/people/injury/research/pub/alcohol-laws/08history/1_introduction.htm

Minnesota Rural Education Association. (2017, October 7). *60 Minnesota school districts to hold referendums*. Minnesota Rural Education Association.

Minor, E. (2015). Classroom composition and racial differences in opportunities to learn. *Journal of Education for Students Placed at Risk (JESPAR), 20*(3), 238–262.

Minor, E. C., Desimone, L. M., Spencer, K., & Phillips, K. J. R. (2015). A new look at the opportunity-to-learn gap across race and income. *American Journal of Education, 121*(2), 241–269.

Mitra, D., Mann, B., & Hlavacik, M. (2016). Opting out: Parents creating contested spaces to challenge standardized tests. *Education Policy Analysis Archives, 24*, 1–23.

Murray, B., Domina, T., Petts, A., Renzulli, L., & Boylan, R. (2020). "We're in this together": Bridging and bonding social capital in elementary school PTOs.

American Educational Research Journal, 54(6). https://doi.org/10.3102/000283
1220908848

National Center for Education Statistics [NCES]. (2010, December). *SLDS technical brief 3: Guidance for statewide longitudinal data systems (SLDS)* (CES 2011-603). Institute of Educational Sciences. https://nces.ed.gov/pubs2011/2011603.pdf

National Center for Education Statistics [NCES]. (2016). Table 216.90. Public elementary and secondary charter schools and enrollment, by state: Selected years, 1999–2000 through 2014–15. Department of Education. Retrieved https://nces.ed.gov/programs/digest/d16/tables/dt16_216.90.asp from

National Center for Education Statistics [NCES]. (2017). Table 203.60. Enrollment and percentage distribution of enrollment in public elementary and secondary schools, by race/ethnicity and level of education. Department of Education. https://nces.ed.gov/programs/digest/d16/tables/dt16_203.60.asp

National Center for Education Statistics [NCES]. (2018). Table 311.40. Percentage of first-year undergraduate students who reported taking remedial education courses, by selected student and institution characteristics: Selected years, 2003–04 through 2015–16. Department of Education. https://nces.ed.gov/programs/digest/d18/tables/dt18_311.40.asp

Ndura, E., Robinson, M., & Ochs, G. (2003). Minority students in high school Advanced Placement courses: Opportunity and equity denied. *American Secondary Education, 32*(1), 21–38.

North Carolina Legislature, (1998). § 95–98.1. Strikes by public employees prohibited (1998).

Nye, B., Konstantopoulos, S., & Hedges, L. V. (2004). How large are teacher effects? *Educational Evaluation and Policy Analysis, 26*(3), 237–257.

Oakes, J. (1985). *Keeping track: How schools structure inequality.* Yale University Press.

Oakes, J., & Guiton, G. (1995). Matchmaking: The dynamics of high school tracking decisions. *American Educational Research Journal, 32*(1), 3–33.

O'Connor, C., Lewis, A., & Mueller, J. (2007). Researching "Black" educational experiences and outcomes: Theoretical and methodological considerations. *Educational Researcher, 36*(9), 541–552.

OECD. (2015). Education at a Glance 2015: OECD indicators. OECD Publishing.

OECD. (2015). Indicator D6: What evaluation and assessment mechanisms are in place? In OECD (Ed.), *Education at a Glance 2015: OECD Indicators.* OECD Publishing.

Office of Civil Rights. (2020). *About IDEA.* U.S. Department of Education.

Omi, M., Nguyen, M. H., & Chan, J. (2020). Panethnicity and ethnic heterogeneity: The politics of lumping and disaggregating Asian Americans and Pacific Islanders in educational policy. In R. T. Teranishi, B. M. D. Nguyen, C. M. Alcantar, & E. R. Curammeng (Eds.), *Measuring race: Why disaggregating data matters for addressing educational inequality* (pp. 46–66). Teachers College Press.

Orfield, G. (1996). The growth of segregation: African Americans, Latinos, and unequal education. In G. Orfield (Ed.), *Dismantling desegregation: The quiet reversal of Brown v. Board of Education,* pp. 53–71. The New Press.

Orfield, G. (2001). *Schools more separate: Consequences of a decade of resegregation.* The Civil Rights Project at UCLA, University of California at Los Angeles.

Orfield, G., & Eaton, S. E. (1996). *Dismantling desegregation. The quiet reversal of Brown v. Board of education.* The New Press.

Orfield, G., & Frankenberg, E. (2013). *Educational delusions? Why choice can deepen inequality and how to make schools fair.* University of California Press.

Orfield, G., & Lee, C. (2005). *Why segregation matters: Poverty and educational inequality.* https://civilrightsproject.ucla.edu/research/k-12-education/integration -and-diversity/why-segregation-matters-poverty-and-educational-inequality /orfield-why-segregation-matters-2005.pdf

Orfield, G., & Lee, C. (2006). *Racial transformation and the changing nature of segregation.* The Civil Rights Project, Harvard University.

Orfield, G., & Lee, C. (2007). *K-12 integration and diversity.* The Civil Rights Project, Harvard University.

Orfield, G., & Yun, J. T. (1999). *Resegregation in American schools.* The Civil Rights Project, Harvard University.

Pannoni, A., & Moody, J. (2019, December 4). IB vs. AP: Discover the differences. *U.S. News and World Report.*

Pappano, L. (2017, January 31). Colleges discover the rural student. *The New York Times.*

Pavel, M., & Curtin, T. (1997). Characteristics of American Indian and Alaska Native Education: Results from the 1990–91 and 1993–94 Schools and Staffing Surveys. U.S. Department of Education.

Penner, A. M., Domina, T., Penner, E. K., & Conley, A. (2015). Curricular policy as a collective effects problem: A distributional approach. *Social Science Research, 52,* 627–641.

Perna, L., & Thomas, S. (2009). Barriers to college opportunity. *Educational Policy, 23*(3), 451–479.

Perry, P. (2002). *Shades of white: White kids and racial identities in high school.* Duke University Press.

Perry, T., Steele, C., & Hilliard, A. G. (2003). *Young, gifted, and Black: Promoting high achievement among African-American students.* Beacon Press.

Phillips, M., & Chin, T. (Eds.). (2004). *School inequality: What do we know?* Russell Sage Foundation.

Plank, S., Schiller, K. S., Schneider, B., & Coleman, J. S. (Eds.). (1993). *Effects of choice in education.* Economic Policy Institute.

Podgursky, M. (2006). Is there a "qualified teacher" shortage? What factors do affect the market for teachers, anyway? *Education Next, 6*(2), 26–33.

Posey-Maddox, L. (2012). Professionalizing the PTO: Race, class, and shifting norms of parental engagement in a city public school. *American Journal of Education, 119*(2), 235–260.

Posey-Maddox, L. (2014). When middle-class parents choose urban schools: Class, race, and the challenge of equity in public education. University of Chicago Press.

Powell, A. J., Farrar, E., Cohen, D. K., National Association of Secondary School Principals (U.S.), & National Association of Independent Schools. Commission on Educational Issues. (1985). *The shopping mall high school: Winners and losers in the educational marketplace.* Houghton Mifflin.

Quillian, L. (2014). Does segregation create winners and losers? Residential segregation and inequality in educational attainment. *Social Problems, 61*(3), 402–426.

Raftery, A. E., & Hout, M. (1993). Maximally maintained inequality: Expansion, reform, and opportunity in Irish education, 1921–75. *Sociology of Education,* 66(1), 41–62.

Rausch, M. K., & Skiba, R. (2004). Disproportionality in school discipline among minority students in Indiana: Description and analysis. Children Left Behind Policy Briefs. Supplementary Analysis 2-A. Center for Evaluation and Education Policy, Indiana University.

Ravitch, D. (2010). *The death and life of the great American school system: How testing and choice are undermining education.* Basic Books.

Ream, R. K. (2003). Counterfeit social capital and Mexican-American underachievement. *Educational Evaluation and Policy Analysis, 25*(3), 237–262.

Reese, W. J. (2001). The origins of progressive education. *History of Education Quarterly, 41*(1), 1–24.

Renzulli, L. A., & Evans, L. (2005). School choice, charter schools, and white flight. *Social Problems, 52*(3), 398–418.

Renzulli, L. A., & Roscigno, V. J. (2005). Charter school policy, implementation, and diffusion across the United States. *Sociology of Education, 78*(4), 344–366.

Riel, V., Parcel, T. L., Mickelson, R. A., & Smith, S. S. (2018). Do magnet and charter schools exacerbate or ameliorate inequality? *Sociology Compass,* e12617.

Rigney, D. (2010). *The Matthew effect: How advantage begets further advantage.* Columbia University Press.

Roda, A., & Wells, A. S. (2012). School choice policies and racial segregation: Where White parents' good intentions, anxiety, and privilege collide. *American Journal of Education, 119*(2), 261–293.

Rosenbaum, J. E. (1976). *Making inequality: The hidden curriculum of high school tracking.* John Wiley & Sons.

Rosenbaum, J. E. (2001). *Beyond college for all: Career paths for the forgotten half.* Russell Sage Foundation.

Rosenholtz, S. J., & Rosenholtz, S. H. (1981). Classroom organization and the perception of ability. *Sociology of Education, 54*(2), 132–140.

Rosenthal, R., & Jacobson, L. (1968). *Pygmalion in the classroom: Teacher expectation and pupils' intellectual development.* Rinehart and Winston.

Sadler, P. M., Sonnert, G., Tai, R. H., & Klopfenstein, K. (Eds.) (2010). *AP: A critical examination of the Advanced Placement program.* Harvard Education Press.

Sanametrix, & American Institutes for Research. (2016, March). *Public-use data file user's manual for the 2013–14 Civil Rights Data Collection.* U.S. Department of Education.

Sattin-Bajaj, C., & Roda, A. (2018). Opportunity hoarding in school choice contexts: The role of policy design in promoting middle-class parents' exclusionary behaviors. *Educational Policy, 34*(7), 992–1035.

Schneider, B., & Stevenson, D. (1999). *The ambitious generation: America's teenagers, motivated but directionless.* Yale University Press.

Shavit, Y., & Blossfeld, H.-P. (1993). *Persistent inequality: Changing educational attainment in thirteen countries. Social Inequality Series.* Westview Press.

Shotton, H. J. (2020). Beyond reservations: Exploring diverse backgrounds and tribal citizenship among Native college students. In R. T. Teranishi, B. M. D. Nguyen, C. M. Alcantar, & E. R. Curammeng (Eds.), *Measuring race: Why disaggregating data matters for addressing educational inequality* (pp. 119–130). Teachers College Press.

Siegel-Hawley, G., Diem, S., & Frankenberg, E. (2018). The disintegration of Memphis-Shelby County, Tennessee: School district secession and local control in the 21st century. *American Educational Research Journal, 55*(4), 651–692.

Skiba, R. J., Horner, R. H., Chung, C.-G., Rausch, M. K., May, S. L., & Tobin, T. (2011). Race is not neutral: A national investigation of African American and Latino disproportionality in school discipline. *School Psychology Review, 40*(1), 85–107.

Skiba, R. J., Michael, R. S., Nardo, A. C., & Peterson, R. L. (2002). The color of discipline: Sources of racial and gender disproportionality in school punishment. *The Urban Review, 34*(4), 317–342.

Smith, A. E., & Crosby, F. J. (2008). From Kansas to Michigan: The path from desegregation to diversity. In G. Adams, M. Biernat, N. R. Branscombe, C. S. Crandall, & L. S. Wrightsman (Eds.), *Decade of behavior commemorating Brown: The social psychology of racism and discrimination* (pp. 99–113). American Psychological Association.

Smith, J., Hurwitz, M., & Avery, C. (2017). Giving college credit where it is due: Advanced Placement exam scores and college outcomes. *Journal of Labor Economics, 35*(1), 67–147.

Snyder, T. D., deBrey, C., & Dillow, S. A. (2019a). *Digest of Education Statistics 2018: 54th Edition*, U.S. Department of Education.

Snyder, T. D., deBrey, C., & Dillow, S. A. (2019b, December). *Digest of Education Statistics 2019: 55th Edition*, U.S. Department of Education.

Sørensen, A. B. (1970). Organizational differentiation of students and educational opportunity. *Sociology of Education, 43*(4), 355–376.

Sørensen, A. B. (1987). The organizational differentiation of students in schools as an opportunity structure. In M. T. Hallinan (Ed.), *The social organization of schools* (pp. 103–129). Springer.

Sørenson, A. B., & Hallinan, M. T. (1977). A reconceptualization of school effects. *Sociology of Education, 50*(4), 273–289.

Southworth, S., & Mickelson, R. A. (2007). The interactive effects of race, gender, and school composition on college track placement. *Social Forces, 86*(2), 497–523.

Stanfield II, J. H. (2008). The gospel of feel-good sociology: Race relations as pseudoscience and the decline in the relevance of American academic sociology in the twenty-first century. In T. Zuberi & E. Bonilla-Silva (Eds.), *White logic, White methods: Racism and methodology* (pp. 271–282). Rowman & Littlefield Publishers.

Stanton-Salazar, R. D., & Dornbusch, S. M. (1995). Social capital and the reproduction of inequality: Information networks among Mexican-origin high school students. *Sociology of Education, 68*(2), 116–135.

Steele, C. M., & Aronson, J. (1995). Stereotype threat and the intellectual test performance of African Americans. *Journal of Personality and Social Psychology, 69*(5), 797–811.

Steers-McCrum, A. R. (2018). Out of the binary and beyond the spectrum: Redefining and reclaiming Native American race. *Critical Philosophy of Race, 6*(2), 216–238.

Steinberg, M. P., & Lacoe, J. (2018). Reforming school discipline: School-level policy implementation and the consequences for suspended students and their peers. *American Journal of Education, 125*(1), 29–77.

Strauss, V. (2016, January 31). The testing opt-out movement is growing, despite government efforts to kill it. *The Washington Post.*

Sutcher, L., Darling-Hammond, L., & Carver-Thomas, D. (2016). A coming crisis in teaching? Teacher supply, demand, and shortages in the U.S. Learning Policy Institute.

Tach, L. M., & Farkas, G. (2006). Learning-related behaviors, cognitive skills, and ability grouping when schooling begins. *Social Science Research, 35*(4), 1048–1079.

Tachine, A. R., Bird, E. Y., & Cabrera, N. L. (2016). Sharing circles: An Indigenous methodological approach for researching with groups of Indigenous peoples. *International Review of Qualitative Research, 9*(3), 277–295.

Tachine, A. R., Cabrera, N. L., & Yellow Bird, E. (2017). Home away from home: Native American students' sense of belonging during their first year in college. *Journal of Higher Education, 88*(5), 785–807.

Teranishi, R. T., Nguyen, B. M. D., Alcantar, C. M., & Curammeng, E. R. (2020). *Measuring race: Why disaggregating data matters for addressing educational inequality.* Teachers College Press.

Tractenberg, P., Roda, A., Coughlan, R., & Dougherty, D. (2020). *Making school integration work: Lessons from Morris.* Teachers College Press.

Tyack, D. B. (1974). *The one best system: A history of American urban education.* Harvard University Press.

Tyson, K. (2011). *Integration interrupted: Tracking, Black students, and acting White after Brown.* Oxford University Press.

U.S. Bureau of Labor Statistics. (2017). *Projections of occupational employment, 2016–26.* Career Outlook.

U.S. Census Bureau. (2017). *SAIPE school district estimates for 2017.* https://www.census.gov/data/datasets/2017/demo/saipe/2017-school-districts.html

U.S. Department of Education [USDOE]. (2004). *NCLB stronger accountability: Testing: Frequently asked questions.* U.S. Department of Education. https://www2.ed.gov/nclb/accountability/ayp/testing-faq.html

U.S. Department of Education [USDOE], (2008). *New race and ethnicity and ethnicity guidance for the collection of federal education data.* https://www2.ed.gov/policy/rschstat/guid/raceethnicity/index.html

U.S. Department of Education [USDOE]. (2015). Improving basic programs operated by local educational agencies (Title I, Part A).

U.S. Department of Education [USDOE]. (2017). *FAQs: Frequently asked questions.* https://www.ed.gov/answers/

U.S. Department of Education [USDOE]. (2020a). *Homeschooling.* https://www.ed.gov/answers/

U.S. Department of Education [USDOE]. (2020b). Every Student Succeeds Act (ESSA): Assessments under Title I, Part A & Title I, Part B: Summary of final regulations. U.S. Department of Education. https://www.ed.gov/essa?src=rn

U.S. Department of Education Office for Civil Rights. (2014, March). *Civil rights data collection data snapshot: Teacher equity.* Civil Rights Data Collection Data Snapshot, Issue 4.

U.S. Department of Justice Civil Rights Division. (2016). U.S. Departments of Education and Justice reach voluntary settlement with Arizona Department of Education to meet the needs of English language learner students. Title VI.

https://www.ed.gov/news/press-releases/us-departments-education-and-justice -reach-voluntary-settlement-arizona-department-education-meet-needs-english -language-learner-students

U.S. Office for Civil Rights. (2017). *Civil rights data collection: Frequently asked questions.* https://www2.ed.gov/about/offices/list/ocr/frontpage/faq/crdc.html

Vanfossen, B. E., Jones, J. D., & Spade, J. Z. (1987). Curriculum tracking and status maintenance. *Sociology of Education, 60*(2), 104–122.

Wachal, R. S. (2000). The capitalization of Black and Native American. *American Speech, 75*(4), 364–365.

Walters, P. B. (2000). The limits of growth. In M. T. Hallinan (Ed.), *Handbook of the sociology of education* (pp. 241–261). Springer.

Wang, W. (2015). *The link between a college education and a lasting marriage.* Pew Research Center. http://www.pewresearch.org/fact-tank/2015/12/04/education -and-marriage/

Weber, K. (2010). Waiting for "SUPERMAN": How we can save America's failing public schools. Public Affairs.

Wells, A. S. (2009). Our children's burden: A history of federal education policies that ask (now require) our public schools to solve societal inequality. In M. A. Rebell & J. R. Wolff (Eds.), *NCLB at the crossroads: Reexamining the federal effort to close the achievement gap* (pp.1–42). Teachers College Press.

Wells, A. S., & Crain, R. L. (1997). *Stepping over the color line: African-American students in White suburban schools.* Yale University Press.

Wildhagen, T. (2014). Unequal returns to academic credentials as a hidden dimension of race and class inequality in American college enrollments. *Research in Social Stratification and Mobility, 38,* 18–31.

Witenko, V., Mireles-Rios, R., & Rios, V. M. (2017). Networks of encouragement: Who's Encouraging Latina/o students and White students to enroll in honors and Advanced-Placement (AP) courses? *Journal of Latinos and Education, 16*(3), 176–191.

Wong, F., & Halgin, R. (2006). The "model minority": Bane or blessing for Asian Americans? *Journal of Multicultural Counseling and Development, 34*(1), 38–49.

Yellow Bird, M. (1999). What we want to be called: Indigenous peoples' perspectives on racial and ethnic identity labels. *American Indian Quarterly, 23*(2), 1–21.

Yosso, T. J. (2005). Whose culture has capital? A critical race theory discussion of community cultural wealth. *Race Ethnicity and Education, 8*(1), 69–91.

Zerquera, D. D., Haywood, J., & DeMucha, M. (2020). More than nuance: Recognizing and serving the diversity of the Latinx community. In R. T. Teranishi, B. M. D. Nguyen, C. M. Alcantar, & E. R. Curammeng (Eds.), *Measuring race: Why disaggregating data matters for addressing educational inequality* (pp. 154–169). Teachers College Press.

Zimmer, R., Gill, B., Booker, K., Lavertu, S., Sass, T. R., & Witte, J. (2009). *Charter schools in eight states: Effects on achievement, attainment, integration, and competition* (Vol. 869). RAND Corporation.

Zuberi, T., & Bonilla-Silva, E. (2008). *White logic, White methods: Racism and methodology.* Rowman & Littlefield Publishers.

Index

Note: Page numbers followed by "*f*" and "*t*" refer to figures and tables; and those followed by "n" indicate notes.

About the Author

Heather E. Price is assistant professor of leadership studies doctoral program with concurrent appointment in the Social, Behavioral, and Forensic Sciences Department at Marian University, where she teaches graduate sociological methods and statistics. Her sociological research agenda on education includes social network analysis in schools, comparing education and education policies at the international level, and analyzing the unforeseen consequences from educational policies.

Price primarily publishes on the sociology of education, including studies on school leadership, school community and climate, teacher commitment, school choice, and social capital among educators. These studies are published in journals such as *American Educational Research Journal, Education Administration Quarterly, Educational Policy, Journal of Educational Administration,* and *Social Science Research* and numerous book chapters on international education and social methods. Price also broadly studies relational sociology, including in her book of *American Generosity: Who Gives and Why?* (Herzog & Price, 2016, Oxford).

Price actively consults for the Organization for Economic Cooperation and Development (OECD) and the International Association for the Evaluation of Educational Achievement (IEA) for the Teaching and Learning International Survey (TALIS), where she works in multination research-policymaker collaborations to design studies, analyze international data, and translate findings into policy recommendations.

Prior to Marian, Price worked as a senior analyst at the University of Notre Dame and in the private educational policy sector as well as teaching for years in Milwaukee Public Schools. While in the private sector, Price worked as a principal investigator for multiyear researcher–practitioner partnerships across public, private, and philanthropic organizations to codesign studies, organize and collect data, analyze results, and interpret findings for practitioners' use.